Published in the United States in 2010 by Mazda Connections

Send correspondence and comments to:

Azarm Ghareman, PhD
c/o Mazda Connections
1241 Johnson Avenue, PMB 118
San Luis Obispo, CA 93401-3306

dr.ghareman@gmail.com

Six Life Secrets of Content Women: A Guide for Emotional Self-Care
Copyright 2010 Azarm Ghareman, PhD

ISBN 0-9745317-3-1

First Edition

Printed in the United States of America
Visit **www.mazdaconnections.com**

Photography: Dr. Jan Simek, Roshan Campbell
Web Design: James Van Lommel
Printed by Poor Richards Press

To My Daughter Roshan

 **Table of Contents**

Six Life Secrets of Content Women

Introduction

Another Self-Help Book?

There is nothing in this book that you don't already know. Should you still read it? That would be like saying if we already know the notes that make up music, should we listen to a new song? We listen to it because of the unique arrangement of its notes and the new emotional place to which it can take us. Furthermore, while reading we can't predict when the wonderful *aha!* moment may occur. So we keep on reading, listening, and tuning in to receive a message at the time we seem most receptive. "When the student is ready, the teacher appears. "

What's Different About This Book?

This is not a self-help book about selecting clothes, appearing slimmer, age-defying skin care, or satisfying your mate in bed. It does not contain quick financial advice, or specific tips on relationships.

Instead, it looks at blocks that prevent a woman from releasing her full energy into her own life.

The six chapters in this book represent a set of principles to help you tap into your deepest energy source; they give you the tools you need to free yourself from the invisible shackles that weigh you down. They can help you identify areas where your emotional energy is being wasted while at the same time they can help you develop a *discipline* to harness your innate energy. You become more content as you are able to achieve more of what you want.

How This Book Came to be

The seed for writing this book has been growing for a number of years. After I divorced and became the single mother of a young child, I began working full time at the local county Mental Health clinic as a Clinical Psychologist while managing a small private practice and teaching a class at a graduate school each year. I enjoyed taking care of my daughter, our home and garden, and took great pride in making homemade meals for us and creating a stable life. Our life was full.

I was often puzzled when I heard the general advice given to women "Make yourself #1 priority," because I didn't know which of my current responsibilities could be given second place: Feeding and caring for my child? Being involved with her school? My work? Housework? Yard work? Paying the bills? Social life? Exercise? I asked in frustration, "Could someone please tell me how to give myself high priority while I still do a good job of everything else that needs to be done?"

As years passed, I learned what it meant to take good care of myself. It wasn't about the occasional manicures or massages, although those felt wonderful at the time. Taking care of myself meant learning to use the limited emotional energy that I had and set better boundaries. Let me share a small example to illustrate this point.

When my daughter was 3-4 years old, she loved when I read stories to her before bedtime. We'd sit on the couch and she'd bring one book after another for me to read. That was our after-bath ritual. Some nights I was tired and didn't feel like reading, but I'd feel bad for wanting to stop because I thought I'd be an inconsistent parent and would harm my child emotionally for life! As months passed, I reasoned with myself and realized that there is a difference between a *rigid* boundary and a *flexible* boundary. A rigid one would be: Read so many stories every night. A flexible boundary would be: Read at least one story every night; more if you are up to it. I started checking in with myself after the first story was finished. My daughter, of course, wanted more. I'd pause to see how I felt. Then I would say: "Mommy can read one more tonight." Some nights I would say: "I am going to finish this story and it's going to be our last one for tonight because I am tired." This is a small, everyday example of how I learned to take care of myself in face of hundreds of daily demands.

With practice, I learned how to organize my time and live my life within my few waking hours so I could do the things that I thought were important for me. I became more *content* with life and gradually achieved even more of what I desired.

Notice, I use the word "content" instead of happy, because the two are not the same. Happiness is a feeling, and therefore can be transient. Contentment is an *attitude*, a lens through which we see our life, and implies a degree of serenity. I became fascinated by what makes a person feel content in life, and began to pay attention to patterns of lifestyle and thoughts that content people have. These people have their share of challenges and disappointments like the rest of us, but they seem to navigate through life holding on to a compass that keeps them on track.

Over the years I continued to work with many women in my role as a psychotherapist. As I listened to them discuss their challenges, I became aware of patterns into which women fall that siphon away their precious energy and make them discontent. I also watched many of my friends feel burdened by the demands of their lives. Many women appeared happy to the world, but when you sat down and listened to their heart, they told you that they were utterly exhausted. I felt compassion for them.

I became determined to write about these patterns as a way to help my fellow sisters. In writing this book, I am also drawing significantly from my own experiences as a woman who has lived in different cultures, as well as watching other people who are content in their lives. All of this weaved together became the text that you are now reading.

Are Women Getting What They Want?

As women, we may look different and have different wishes, but we all share the same fundamental needs: we need to know that someone loves and respects us; we need food, shelter and enough money for necessities; we want to feel productive, and we need to know that we make a difference in life. These are our needs.

What are our wants? Nearly all of us want to be healthy, live a financially secure life, and have satisfying relationships with friends and family. Just about all of us know at an intellectual level what we need to do to achieve all three, but clearly not all of us can do that to the extent that we want. Many of us have dozens of cookbooks: low fat, low cholesterol, vegetarian, but does that mean we have solved our overeating problem? Even more than cookbooks, we have a collection of self-help books about communication, parenting and relationships. Does that mean we know how to build and maintain a low conflict relationship with those around us? If we are honest the answer is no to both of these questions.

We often start with good intentions and make plans for what we want to accomplish, but soon other things begin to interfere and we lose focus and momentum. This means that many of our projects never get completed, or if they do, the results do not last. Remember that we lead incredibly stressful lives; we tolerate daily commutes; juggle conflicting demands, and have a limited amount of time and energy to do what needs to be done. No wonder we lose focus.

In addition to the external demands that we face because of our roles, we put further pressure on ourselves. For example, we listen to cultural messages that tell us we should turn back the clock and regain our body of youth or else face social disapproval. Another source of pressure is the fact that the lion share of the responsibility to keep the flame of passion alive in our romantic relationships seems to be on us. We listen to programs and read articles that teach us the latest tips on how keep this flame alive.

Although our mates may help us around the house, the majority of us who work outside the home find that we are primarily the ones responsible to make the domestic wheels run smoothly. Just watch what happens in any household with children when the mother is gone for over a week. Living can become an exhausting proposition. Is this what we wanted? Work more and be less content?

What's Going on?

Maybe we are exhausted because we women have been socially programmed to give until we feel depleted. Is there a way we can take care of others as well as ourselves? Is something preventing us from getting what we want? If we truly desire something in our life, what is it that stands in the way? It is as if some of us carry an invisible *shackle* that drags us down and sabotages us. We may be completely unaware of this. Sometimes these shackles are repetitive thoughts, feelings, beliefs or habits. They tie us down, sap our energy, and will not leave us alone unless we untangle ourselves from them—and that can only happen when we have both the necessary information *and* the discipline to apply what we know.

The six chapters in this book are created as responses to those shackles.

Is This Book for You?

This book is written for women from many walks of life. As a woman maybe,

- You are in midlife and face an empty nest with a broken heart and need to rediscover who you are.
- You want to learn how to take care of yourself without appearing selfish to others.
- You want to feel better about yourself and stop a self-defeating habit.
- You are a working mother and spouse, and want to organize your time to have a more balanced life.
- You are a working mother and feel as if you are losing yourself to everyone else's needs around you.
- You are in your 30's and wonder what you should do with your life now that your only child is old enough to go to school during the day.
- You want to select mates who are kinder to you in your relationships.

- You may wonder why, given your talent and ambition, you have not achieved your peak in life.
- You may wish to gather enough motivation to get in better physical shape, or follow your lifelong dream.
- You are tired of someone else holding the remote control to your life. You want to claim your power back.
- You are just starting your adult life and don't want to repeat the expensive mistakes of others around you. You want to start off on a fresh path.

You may be at a stage in your life where a particular chapter interests you more than another, or you may come back to a topic after a few months and feel ready to digest the information at that time. Once you learn to practice the set of skills offered in each chapter, it will be easier to stay focused on what you want because you'll have a compass to guide you.

No woman I know has mastered all six of these principles, but many practice a number of them successfully. When I talk to a content woman who has accomplished a lot in her life by her own standards, I feel like I am in the company of someone who is neither burdened nor consumed by life. This woman has some creative energy left at the end of the day, and she radiates optimism with a sense of comfort about who she is.

What does she do differently?

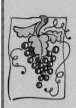

Chapter 1

Close the
All-You-Can-Eat 24-Hour Buffet

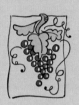

In my private practice, the essence of my work with nearly every woman eventually becomes helping her develop stronger boundaries and set better limits. Even women who appear assertive and confident in a work setting can have difficulty saying "no" in the context of a personal relationship.

Setting healthy boundaries is the hallmark of taking good care of ourselves--and this eventually leads to greater contentment.

In an attempt to be nurturing and loving, many of us give to our mates, to our children, to our careers, and to our friends as if there is no end to our energy supply—our buffet is kept open 24-hours a day. Of course no one complains about this generous giving. And why should they? They are accustomed to having their needs met on demand because *we have already established the pattern.*

Is There a Problem With Giving Too Much?

What is "too much" varies greatly for each person. Some women give generously to others without neglecting themselves, or without developing resentment in the long run. In their case, it is hard to see a downside to their giving. On the other hand, the majority of us give at the expense of taking care of ourselves; we gradually deplete our energy; lose our sense of humor, tenderness, and stunt our creative spirit. We take away from ourselves to give to others—and that can become a wellness issue for us in the long run. This pattern has consequences for others in the family as well. It can slow down the maturity rate of our children as we keep softening their landings. Furthermore, it sets a poor example for our children: It teaches them not to value themselves or their mother. This is probably the opposite of what every woman wishes for her children.

The short answer to the question is: "Yes, there is a problem with giving too much. It drains our energy. We become less content as time passes." Our children end up with an unhappy mother.

Have You Been Running a 24-Hour Buffet?

Finding out whether you are among the millions of women who give too much is not as easy as identifying whether you have osteoporosis or anemia. There are no blood tests or x-rays to take. Many women who give too much are actually praised as *good moms* and *devoted wives*. As I said earlier, no one complains about having 24-hour room service. Therefore, the problem remains masked for a long time. Over time though, other symptoms develop that indicate we are giving beyond our emotional means.

If you are feeling brave, here are some difficult questions to sincerely ask yourself:

1) Has it been a long time since you have taken an overnight trip with your spouse and gone away somewhere?
2) Has it been a long time since you have taken an overnight trip with a girl friend and gone away somewhere?
3) Do you prepare more than one version of a meal to please your family's taste at the table, essentially turning into a short-order cook?
4) Do you skip your workouts because of your family's hectic life and obligations?

5) Do you cut the crust off the children's sandwiches before packing them in the lunch boxes?

6) When you come home tired, does your family run to you with demands just when you want to collapse and relax for a while?

7) Do you secretly wish someone would take your family away for a long weekend and leave you home alone?

8) Do you have a growing list of unfinished projects?

9) Are you the one who makes all the preparations for a weekend get-away with your romantic partner?

10) Do you let your children negotiate with you endlessly before you eventually give in?

11) After giving the standard line "I am happily married and love my children", do you actually admit that you are exhausted and overwhelmed at the end of the day because of all you have to do as a woman?

12) Do you often get easily irritable and fatigued?

13) Do you feel life is passing you by?

14) Are you sleep-deprived?

15) Do you find it challenging to keep a balance between work, family, and play?

16) Do you know more about what you have in your pantry than in your (or your joint) retirement account?

17) Do you know what your credit score is?

18) Do you find it hard to pursue your favorite hobby?

19) Do you tend to choose mates who, in general, do not reciprocate your giving in the relationship? Do you feel short-changed?

20) Are you reluctant to allow yourself an occasional *black* period (no cell phone, no phone, no email)?

21) Do you find it hard to tell the babysitter that you are going out and that you cannot be reached for the evening?

22) Do you work more than 40 hours a week without getting overtime?

23) Do you feel awkward giving yourself a monthly salary for the house/yard work you do?

24) Do you find it difficult to break a relationship that you know is emotionally toxic for you?

25) Do you avoid saying, "No, I'm not interested?"

26) Does it bother you to delegate and accept the outcome?

If you have said "yes" to more than 7-8 questions, take a deep breath! You are not alone. Millions of sisters across the nation share your challenge. Sit back and enjoy the rest of the material in this chapter, which is intended to help you, not add to your guilt.

Why Do We Give Too Much?

This is a complex question and deserves a book of its own for a just answer. For our purpose, we can summarize a few of the main reasons. The typical answer is "because we are socially conditioned to give a lot", but let us remember that a virus attacks a receptive host!

After a meeting, a woman came up to me one day and said that she gets home at 6:30 p.m., and by the time she puts dinner on the table and helps her kids, the evening is over. She doesn't have time to go for a walk or do anything for herself. She has developed numerous health issues and looks visibly run down. "I don't know how to take care of myself. Period." I was struck by her honesty, and felt compassion for her. She spoke for millions of women across the country. What is happening here?

The real question is why do *some* women give so much that it ends up hurting their life? There are many reasons but here are some of the most common:

#1) A woman may want to feel needed. It is only human to want to feel important and needed, but when a person gets a lot of her self-worth from other people's feedback, then problems can develop. A woman, who gives to others when in fact she wants to receive, is only masking her deeper needs. It is better in the long run for her to identify those needs and find a way to satisfy them without depleting her energy.

#2) A woman may be postponing her own journey in life. This can be especially true for a woman who prolongs her role as a mother by over-functioning for her children. If she admits that as her children grow her services as a mother decrease, then she has to face the challenge of finding her own path in life. This can be anxiety-provoking if she has spent years of playing Chutes and Ladders, watching Elmo, or driving junior to soccer games. She has to retrain herself for new employment and opportunities.

#3) A woman may be striving to restore her broken parent. Unfortunately this is a common scenario. Daughter is raised in a family where mother or father had many problems of their own and she ended up taking care of her needs as well as the parent's needs. When she is older, she continues to select mates, bosses, and friends who are needy. With a pattern that is well rehearsed, she gives generously until she is burned out.

#4) A woman keeps hoping that others reciprocate and love her in return. Women who had a deprived childhood or a poor relationship with their mother often want to compensate and give their children what they themselves didn't have. This can be positive in some cases. For example, Debra was raised in a small town with few educational opportunities. She lost her mother at the tender age of 6 and was raised by her aunt. When she had a family of her own, education became a high priority. She'd rather spend money on piano lessons and math tutors than on fancy stereo equipment or plush furniture.

On the other hand, some compensate by becoming too involved in their children's lives— enmeshed—and basically try to give their children the mother they never had. Bad idea! Such a woman would benefit more by giving *herself* the love she never had and by mothering *herself* first.

#5) A woman may feel guilty for working outside the home. Guilt is the motivator behind many of our behaviors, and a number of working women feel utterly guilty about being away from their family. They compensate by catering to every need of their child or teen, or they try to compensate for their absence by buying things. It is hard to set limits when guilt is in charge of the remote control in life. I have heard from numerous women that because they work full-time, they feel they shouldn't go out as a couple or do something by themselves in the evenings or even on weekends.

#6) A woman may be making up for a child's absent or marginal father. It is a sad fact that many women fulfill the role of both parents for their children, and these women end up performing double tasks. It becomes especially important for these women to recognize that they are crossing the line and giving too much of themselves because they are a vulnerable group to catch the virus! For example, they might have a harder time finding someone to care for their children so they can get away for a night with a friend.

#7) A woman may not trust the quality of the work done by others, so she takes charge and stays in charge. This is a full-proof recipe for becoming overwhelmed, both at work and at home. Perfectionism imprisons a woman to a lifestyle of endless chores and little play. These women often angrily criticize how their mates work in the kitchen; disapprove of the help of cleaning services; dislike co-workers' performances, and clean children's rooms after the children have attempted to clean it themselves. "So I might as well do it myself and save time in the long run", becomes the motto. They eventually become resentful, depressed, and unhappy.

Tips on How to Limit the Hours and Service of the 24-Hour Buffet

Relax. You don't have to suddenly close the buffet, but you can start by offering fewer items on the menu and limiting the operating hours. How does this translate into your life? Let's go back to the list of questions you asked yourself and answer some of them.

Question: Has it been a long time since you have taken an overnight trip with a girl friend and gone away somewhere?

Recommendation: Let's assume that you have a family and the budget is limited. It may not be feasible to make an out of town trip in addition to the family trips. What you can do is to go to a friend's home overnight who lives in town, perhaps with another friend or two, and have a blast! Enjoy an evening of girl talk, drink, food, painting nails, watching a movie, and let your hostess fix you a lovely breakfast. Return home the next day relaxed.

When it is your turn to reciprocate, choose a night when your kids are at a slumber party and your house is empty. This strategy allows you to nurture your adult-female connections at little cost.

Question: Do you prepare more than one version of a meal to please your family's taste at the table, essentially becoming a short order cook?

Recommendation: If you are doing this, my heart goes out to you because you have created a monster of a job for yourself, which is going to take some time to undo.

Most women have good intentions and want their family to eat what they like. However, what these women may not realize is that they are not doing their children any favor by giving them the message that the children can have their way in life.

Clearly, not everyone around the table is going to like or eat everything that you fix. You need to fix <u>one</u> menu per meal and let them figure out how much to eat. No other alternatives. No getting up and heating a burrito in the microwave if they don't like your dish. It would help tremendously if your mate supported you in this endeavor. As you plan your menu, you can get some input from your family each night in the following way:

Ask one child to choose one vegetable (give him choices if you want)
Ask another child to pick the starch (pasta, potato, rice, etc)
Ask another family member how to cook the starch? (Mashed, baked, spaghetti, etc.)
Ask another family member what kind of salad dressing for the night they like.
Let the pickiest family member help you in the kitchen by preparing the item he/she has picked.
Ask the children to find a new vegetable to pick each week. Reward them for their ideas, Go on-line and find recipes for them and even build your meals around their idea.

Tell your family that if everyone cooperates throughout the week, each Saturday, you'll fix their favorite meal and dessert.

Question: Do you skip your workouts because of your family's hectic life and obligations?

Recommendation: We get upset at our spouses who seem to find time to play golf when we easily give up our workout time in exchange for family obligations, kids' homework, and carpools. It's a self-inflicted wound and we need to find a way to stop it because our health is at risk.

Ladies, if you have to beg, borrow, and steal, find 30-45 minutes to work out daily regardless of what is happening. Get up early, walk at lunch time, jump rope while you talk with your kids, take the kids out for a walk and ask about their day, buy a few weights and lift them in your bedroom as the kids do their homework. Do not accept any excuses. In other chapters of this book you will find tips on how to organize your time and make a commitment to wellness so your journey will become smoother.

Question: Do you cut the crust off the children's sandwiches before packing their lunch boxes?

Recommendation: Cutting off the crust is not the same as cutting up an apple for a two year old so he doesn't choke. Cutting the crust is entering the slippery slope of moms who cut the crust off today, peel the apple tomorrow, take the bruise off the peach the next day, and who knows where it eventually ends.

Don't distort the food. If you have been cutting the crust off, slice the sandwich diagonally in half and let your child cut the crust off himself. You can use the strength-based approach by saying: "You are now old enough to take the crust off yourself." They'll get tired of picking the crust after a week and start eating the whole thing.

Question: Do you know more about what you have in your pantry than in your (or your joint) retirement account?

Recommendation: You may wonder why this question or the one about the credit score are included in the list. The reason is that financial savvy offers a degree of freedom to a woman, and when a woman doesn't know what her credit score or retirement composition is, she is walking in darkness, or leaning on others. She is either doing so much for others that she doesn't have time to pay attention to her financial life, or she has become excessively dependent on and trusting of others. Neither of them is a good sign.

Make time to find out your score and retirement profile. Get educated and stay educated. It takes 10 minutes a month to review a financial statement.

Question: Has it been a while since you found time to pursue your favorite hobby?

Recommendation: It is understandable that a woman with a few young children has little time to do anything but care for them and the necessities of the home, but there are many women who continue to ignore their passion for their hobbies when the children go off to school. They say: "I *used to* sew or write or paint".

The point is that we need to feed our creativity at every stage of life. Creativity can be achieved through music, writing, cooking, dance, decoration, athletics, painting--anything that involves creating something that didn't exist before, and which gives you pleasure.

You might say there is no time, or you might feel guilty taking time from your family for pursuing a hobby. Remember that the time you invest in your hobby is being invested in the mother of the family. What better gift than giving a content mother to a family? If you feel you don't have the time, schedule the time, and you *will* find more.

Question: Do you tend to choose mates who, in general, do not reciprocate your giving in the relationship? Do you feel short-changed?

Recommendation: This is a frequent complaint of millions of women who are in a committed relationship. They carry hurt, anger, and resentment. Again, an entire book can be written about this topic, but let us be brief and focus on the main reasons why this might happen.

Remember, reciprocity is not the same as symmetry. He doesn't have to do the same things for you, but it is nice if he *reciprocates* in other ways.

a) Some women find their mates don't give back as much because the women are actually giving <u>too</u> much and their expectations are unreasonable. This is where you need to cut back and invest some of that kindness in yourself and others. Bring some balance into the relationship and you might be happier, not because he is giving more, but because you are giving less!

b) Another reason might be a woman who chooses men who are emotionally aloof, unavailable, and plain cold and then wonders why they don't give back to her. She needs to look at her family of origin and see where that pattern was established, and how that pattern is serving her needs. Do aloof men protect her from becoming too intimate and vulnerable in a relationship?

This might begin a long journey of self-discovery for her and may even require the support of a professional along the way.

Question: Do you work more than 40 hours a week without getting overtime?

Recommendation: This question is a good blood test for owners of a 24-hour buffet! You are basically telling your employer: "Go ahead, use me as you wish. I won't complain. I don't know my worth." You may have a responsible job, but what *motivates* you to put in more hours without compensation?

The way I see it, there are two solutions. If the company doesn't pay overtime, and you still have to work overtime at times, use comp time and take time off at your convenience, or leave after your work hours end and respect your boundaries.

Question: Do you find it hard to tell the babysitter that you are going out and that you cannot be reached for the evening?

Recommendation: Ah, the curse of cell phones and text messaging. Motherhood has been glorified in the last 20 to 30 years to a point where many women feel sinful if they break contact, even for an hour, with junior.

It is absolutely necessary for children to experience your physical absence. The opportunity gives them several emotional states to work through, and by the time you come back, they are ready to greet you with an "I love you Mommy" drawing.

Tell your babysitter the rules about emergency and whom to call (911, grandma, neighbor, and pediatrician). Then leave. Turn off the phone and say you'll be back at a certain time. If your child is sick and you want to find out about the status, tell the babysitter: "I'll call you at 8:30 p.m." Keep the phone off the rest of the night. If there is an emergency, she'll go down the list and make calls.

You need breaks.

Question: Do you avoid saying: "No, I'm not interested?"

Recommendation: As I was writing this chapter, I kept track of the requests made of me during one week.

Would you like to buy Girl Scout cookies?

Would you like to donate to the Police and Children's fund?

Would you like to sign a petition for xxx Initiative?

Would you like to try a sample of xxx's new fragrance?

Would you be interested in buying the extended warranty for the printer? (Asked 3 times)

Can you join our book club this year?

Would you like to join our Sunday walk group?

Would you like to have dinner on Friday?

Can I get a ride from you to my mechanic?

Can we buy a dog? A hamster? Please!

I said "no" to all of them except the one about taking my friend to the mechanic shop without feeling guilty. The trick is to pause and ask yourself whether the offer is right for *you*, and if the request is coming from a friend, will accepting it make your friendship stronger? For example, the friend who invited me to the book club is rather opinionated and rigid about controversial issues. I don't think it would serve our friendship in the long run if I increase my contact with her in such a context. Saying "no" was the right thing.

Another example is saying "no" to the walking group. I like them, but they love to chat constantly as they walk, and I like to ponder and relax. I decided to continue my solitary walks and visit them some other time.

And when my daughter asks me for the 178th time whether she can have a dog, I say: "That's a closed issue." Do not engage in endless talk if someone should already anticipate your answer. It all comes back to maintaining healthy boundaries.

If you find a soft and kind way to respond and say "no" to someone, you not only will not offend them, you may actually help preserve your relationship with them. Remember, had I said "yes" to the book club friend, I would have drifted away from her within a few months.

What about feeling guilty about saying "no" to charity? I choose what charity to contribute, not the solicitor. Police fund is not one of them. End of story.

Question: Does it bother you to delegate and accept the outcome?

Recommendation: This question relates to several others in the list: Are you sleep deprived? Do you get irritable? Do children run to you the moment you get home? Do you wish for a weekend by yourself? A "yes" answer to any of these indicates a woman who is doing too much, and probably not asking often enough for help.

I think we are talking about an efficient woman who gets things done and can't stand waiting around for someone to "get around to doing the dishes later in the day." Such a woman does a great job of running the household, carpooling, keeping a social calendar, keeping doctors' appointments, ballet and karate lessons, and I almost forgot, work full-time outside the home. Yes, she can. But she is paying for it by her blood.

Ladies, don't let your mates and children slide just because they don't do things your way or up to your standards. Remove the incentive for poor performance. Teach them 2-3 meals and then ask them to make them occasionally. Teach them; supervise them; go away; come back and inspect. If you child has not done it according to expectation you can say: "That was a good try. Looks like you could use more practice. How about doing the dishes tomorrow night too?"

I remember asking my daughter to help me rake leaves for half an hour. Well, she was young and got tired after ten minutes and wanted to go back inside. "This is boring." I changed my strategy and instead of paying her by the hour I said: "Each time you fill the bucket with leaves, you get a $1." Want to bet how quickly she raked the leaves that day?

Be happy to get pink slips from your family members as they become capable of doing more. Of course that won't happen until you pull back and do *less*.

P.S. Please stop telling them to wear their jackets when they go out! If they get cold, they'll take care of themselves.

Where Do We Go From Here?

Let's assume that you have been honest in identifying yourself as the owner of a 24-hour buffet and would like to take steps to help the situation. Here are a few reminders:

    a) It has taken years to get to where you are. It is unrealistic to expect to change over a week or a month. Give yourself time and space and take easy steps. This will give you and your family time to adjust to change so you all can grow together—not apart.

b) Pick an item from the list of your "yes" answers that seems most practical to you at this time. Build success and move on to select another one.

c) As you change a behavior, your family may not like it. What? No more room service? Be ready for some whining or guilt-inducing backlash. Hang in there. Stay steady.

d) Find a friend who is stronger than you and supports your growth. You are going to need it.

What if You Feel Guilty About Limiting the 24-Hour Buffet?

You might as well count on it. Keep in mind that we have evolved to care for our children, and those little monsters (bless their hearts) have evolved to suck every ounce of energy from us. The moment we give less, the red light of guilt goes on in our body. This is nature's way of ensuring that mother bear is not abandoning the little cub. Remember how guilty you felt when you went out to dinner and little daughter was crying at the door? That means both you and she were following nature's script to the letter. Nonetheless, it doesn't mean that you must listen and stay home, never take a class, or be available all the time.

*　　*　　*　　*

 Nourish yourself and what you offer others will be a
wonderful gift. The best gift to give a child is
a happy mother.

Content women focus on wellness, not thinness.

They perceive taking good care of themselves as an ethical responsibility toward their community, and not as a self-serving act. They practice the discipline of taking care of themselves, which means that even when they don't feel like doing something one day, they do it out of devotion and commitment to their wellness.

*   *   *   *   *

As I write the outline for this chapter, there are three weeks to Thanksgiving, and most of the women's and cooking magazines are devoted to decadent holiday recipes and decorations promised to be better than last year's. At the same time many magazine editors seem seriously worried about us overeating. They have included articles that teach us how to make better choices and control our portions so we can move away from the table before we completely lose control. Maybe these editors have reason to be worried. It has been estimated that the average American gains 7-9 lbs during the holidays. After the holidays the magazine issues will focus on dieting and exercise tips to take off the pounds we have gained. This cycle of feast and diet repeats every year.

Surely, there is a less contentious way to relate to food, not just at holiday time but all year long.

Is food our friend or foe?

The majority of us find our relationship to food extraordinarily challenging. Most women are dissatisfied with their weight, and many are down right depressed about it. Some of us have become afraid of food and believe that it is more powerful than we are. We say: "I better not get near the buffet table", or "Don't offer me that. If I start eating one, I'll want the whole package." The implication is that *food* is in charge—is the Master—and we are the powerless slaves. We have completely lost faith in our ability to feed ourselves in a sensible way, and have arrived at a point where we need experts to tell us what we should eat, what time of the day, in what combination, and of course, how much. This further diminishes our sense of power and self-esteem.

We can learn to befriend food again, and this chapter offers some practical tips to achieve that.

What is Wellness?

Many years ago I worked at a nationwide weight loss center and counseled women who wanted to lose weight. I saw that most women could indeed lose weight, but the real challenge was keeping it off. Week after week as I listened to the women's stories and struggles, it became clear to me that many of them needed help in developing greater *discipline* to change their lifestyles to maintain the weight loss.

But weight loss and maintenance are only a part of caring for ourselves. *Wellness* is the larger picture that emerges from the balance of <u>all</u> of the following parts:

29

- ❖ Healthy eating
- ❖ Movement and activity
- ❖ Sleep hygiene
- ❖ Stress Management
- ❖ Social and spiritual enrichment

A person can have an ideal body weight but have poor eating habits, sleep inadequately and lead a lifestyle that is devoid of emotional nourishment. This person is not on the wellness path.

We spend millions of dollars each year on diet plans, exercise programs, nutritional supplements, self-help books and seminars. This chapter is not offering more information on nutrition or exercise. There is already abundant information available through experts' books and the media about making better food choices, incorporating exercise into our daily life, and many other health-related topics. Lack of knowledge is not the issue here; what's missing is the ability to apply what we already know to our lives. The question worth asking is, "What is standing in our way?"

What is the shackle that is dragging us down?

I believe there are two main reasons why some of our attempts at fitness or weight management may not be fully successful.

#1 Multi-dimensional approach

Many of us have adopted a reductionistic attitude toward wellness. We want to lose weight but we forget that wellness is a holistic term and needs to be approached from many dimensions. We set ourselves up for failure when we zero in on a *part* rather than the *whole*. Does this mean we need to bring all of the five dimensions of our wellness under control at once? Of course not. That would be overwhelming. But it does mean that if we start in the area of weight management, we need to keep in mind that there are other equally important factors that we need to consider before our plan succeeds. For example, if I am chronically sleep-deprived, I'll become sluggish and irritable the next day and will be tempted to reach for easy, sweet snacks at work. My weight management plan is not going to be effective because I have sabotaged it.

Another example would be a social life that makes a woman feel alone, bored, and unstimulated. Although Melanie does her best to watch what she eats during the day at the office, she occupies her evening by watching television, surfing the Internet and snacking in solitude. She is not happy about this situation. Her efforts are not likely to pay off until she takes her total health into consideration. The social and spiritual dimensions of her life need as much nourishment as her physical body.

#2 Commitment to Wellness.

The second reason I believe many of us struggle with reaching our desired fitness level is because of the casual attitude we show toward wellness. Casual? Aren't we actually obsessed with fitness in this culture?

Let's take dating as an example. When a woman casually dates a man, she is continually gathering information about him and deciding whether to pursue the relationship further. This can go on for months or even years. Her date may show characteristics that turn her off, after which she says: "He is not the right man for me. I don't want to pursue this much longer." The relationship ends. On the other hand, her relationship might deepen and get to a point where she decides to go steady and eventually make a commitment to this person--a serious commitment, like marriage. Once she makes the decision, she will not go back and forth on that decision anymore when small conflicts surface between the two of them. She has made a commitment to him and will stick to it through thick and thin.

Yes, many of us do have a casual attitude toward wellness. We tend to follow our wellness plans on certain days of the week, when we are mostly eating at home, when we are not under too much stress at work, when we are not traveling, when we don't have company visiting us, or when the sun is shining. These may be our favorite, time-tested habits, but they are not going to help us reach our goal.

When you become serious about taking good care of yourself, you need to make a <u>commitment</u> to Wellness. Period. Marry the idea. Don't just casually date it!

What Does it Mean to Take Care of Ourselves?

For many of us this means getting a facial or a massage or buying some flowers. Those are certainly pleasurable activities and have their place when it comes to pampering ourselves. But taking care of ourselves at a deep level means giving ourselves a high priority and making a serious commitment to our wellness.

Many of us are deeply devoted to our family and friends and we take our role as nurturers seriously. What often happens is that at any given moment, the need of a child, a mate, a co-worker or a friend becomes more important than ours. Christopher needs help with homework; you stay at the office late to help the boss with a project; Madison has soccer practice; Church needs help with the bake sale; husband's father is ill and needs food delivered to him. We immediately lower ourselves a few notches on the priority list and take care of their needs. As you all know, the needs of those around us are not going to stop.

Here is the important question: Is there a way we can care for those we love *and* keep ourselves on top of the priority list? The answer is "Of course!"

Get Used to the Idea.

Many of us feel guilty about saying that we should have high priority. We have been socially brought up to be caretakers, and it is no wonder that we mistake caring for ourselves with being selfish. How far will a car travel on an empty tank? Not very far, and that's exactly the case with a woman at the core of a household on whom many depend. She can't offer much to others on an empty tank. The paradox is that the more we nourish ourselves, the more energy we have available to help others. So much for being selfish!

A number of women who took me into their confidence said they are afraid that if they begin to take care of themselves, "they will drift away from their spouses." This is an intriguing statement. I have seen women who react to years of resentment by pushing their family away and claiming their freedom. That is not the path I am suggesting here. I advocate a loving approach that brings you even closer to your family by making you more content in the long run.

Plan Ahead.

Those of you who have raised a baby can relate to this example. Remember each time you left the house you made sure you had baby food and a diaper with you? You were able to do that unapologetically because your baby had a high priority at that time, and no matter what else was happening, you took care of your baby's needs by planning ahead.

The only way you can promptly respond to others' demands as they emerge *and* keep yourself as a high priority is to have a plan of action already in place for yourself. Not having a plan for what you are going to eat or when you are going to exercise on a given day can leave you tempted to eat impulsively, postpone exercise, and run yourself to the ground as you get stressed.

Example #1

Michelle is single and in her 40's. Lately she has been working late at the real estate office, and by the time she comes home around 7 or 8 p.m., she is so tired she does not feel like cooking. She snacks during the afternoon at work and says she doesn't need dinner. However, she continues to graze at home and has a late night binge. She wants to ride her stationary bike at night, but that rarely happens. She blames herself for not having enough will power but does not know how to break the cycle. This situation can be improved by any of the following:

- First of all, Michelle needs to make a commitment and spend some time planning for her wellness.

- Michelle can redefine the concept of dinner. Dinner doesn't have to be a hot meal as she used to have before. She can shift the bulk of her food to breakfast and lunch and consider snacks such as yogurt, fruit, nuts, or low-fat cheese as her evening meal.

- Knowing how tired and stressed she feels when she gets home, Michelle can listen to calming music on her commute. A more relaxed Michelle is less apt to graze and binge under stress.

- If she likes the traditional idea of dinner, she can pack a nutritious dinner and take it to work. She can eat it before she returns home.

- Michelle can mark off a few blocks of time a week on her schedule for exercise. She probably should not rely on exercising after work because that could easily be sabotaged. Morning or a lunchtime walk might be more realistic. Weekends would be another good option.

Example #2

Heather is in her 20's, newly married, and works full time at a pediatric dental office. She is taking some evening classes as a preparation to enter a graduate dental program. She has been incredibly stressed lately trying to keep a balance between work, new marriage, social life, and schoolwork. She and her husband have been relying on take-out or frozen food, which has been hard on their limited budget. Heather has not found time to swim as she did before and finds that upsetting also. She used to enjoy cooking a great deal, but, "who can think of cooking when classes end at 9 p.m. three nights a week?" Her husband wants to help but knows nothing about cooking. The situation is putting stress on their tender marriage.

This example clearly shows how all five areas of wellness in Heather's life are beginning to suffer. Here are some suggestions:

- Perhaps it was a mistake for Heather to give up cooking, especially since she enjoyed it so much. She can devote 1-2 hours each weekend and prepare several meals for the week and freeze them. This will ensure a healthy and less costly meal plan.

- Heather and her husband can plan for the nights that she arrives late. Dinner can be one of the (defrosted) meals she has prepared the weekend before, or she can put soup or stew ingredients in a crock-pot in the morning and come home to a delicious meal at night. Little by little she can teach her husband to prepare simple meals, but that is a project for the coming months.

- Three days a week are her longest days. She can go on a brisk walk during lunch. She can do it alone to relax, go with a friend or her husband as a way to socialize.

- Time is precious for Heather. She needs to take a hard look at her list of *should and ought to's* and postpone a few things until her classes are over, otherwise her stress level will continue to be intolerable. For example, she doesn't have to return every email and phone call right away, she doesn't have to keep a spotless home, nor does she have to say, "yes" to every request coming her way.

Don't Give the Car Keys to a Child!

It might be helpful to visualize a child within us who nags us for a midnight cookie, who can't say no to a second helping of dessert, and who doesn't want to go on a walk with us. None of us would dream of opening the garage door and giving our car keys to a four year old, yet when we sneak into the kitchen at night and eat cookies in the dark, or talk ourselves out of a walk, we are giving the keys of our wellness to the four year old in us.

We need to remember that *we* are the adults, and we need to start making conscious choices about our wellness. The child will continue to make her demands or throw tantrums, but it is up to us to speak kindly to her just as we would to a real child. Being a good mother to that child means giving her what she *needs* in the long run—not what she thinks she wants at the moment. We have to start saying "no" to her in a kind way.

- Next time you are tempted to stay home instead of going out to walk, say kindly to your *child*: "Let's go play. It'll make us both feel better afterwards."

- When you want seconds and thirds, take a breath and tell your *child*: "Sweetie: you've have enough for one day. You can have more next time this is served. Let's enjoy the company of our friends."

- When you come home tired and want a quick fix, tell your *child*: "I can tell you are tired. I am going to do something that will actually help relax you", then proceed to do something relaxing like taking a bath or listening to music.

- When your *child* beats herself up and says she's been bad for overeating, tell her: " Hey, You are the only one I've got. I love you no matter what you eat!"

Reframe Your Weight Not as a Problem but as a Blessing.

I am one of those people who have to watch what they eat or else I gain weight easily. For a long time I thought of this as a nuisance and wished I could eat anything without gaining weight like some of my friends. One day, I had an epiphany.

Most of you are familiar with the smell of the home cooking gas-butane. Of course, natural butane is odorless, but for safety reasons an odor is added to it to alert us when there is a gas leak. I view my tendency to gain weight as the "alarming odor of butane" in that it warns me that I am eating too much. Otherwise, I'd be making gastronomic suicide, quietly developing health problems such as diabetes, high cholesterol, and not even know about it. This attitude shift has made a difference in how I view weight gain and weight management.

Treat yourself with honor.

We all have seen before and after pictures of women who have lost a lot of weight and are understandably proud of their accomplishment. Each time I have seen someone talk about their before-and-after looks, the person seems to be somewhat ashamed of the overweight self and jubilant about the thinner version. The implicit assumption is that the thinner version is superior. It is as if we want to hide the larger version of ourselves in the closet and throw away the keys. I believe that this attitude can be damaging to our efforts in the long run. We will most likely feel guilty for the way we have treated the large one and we'll go looking for her and bring her back to our life. The weight will come back, plus the guilt.

We need to honor ourselves regardless of our size. The large version of us was doing the best that she could with the tools that were available to her at the time. We need not put her down or be ashamed of her. It is best to part with her in an honorable way.

Commitment to Wellness is a form of Deep Self-Love.

Chapter 3 Live Frugally

Frugal living is at the core of a content life just as a seed is the center of the life of a fruit. A frugal woman has learned to tap into the abundance and simplicity of life and feels satisfied with what she has.

Who is considered Frugal?

It is not always simple to define a frugal person. Take Amy and Katherine as examples. Amy shops at the local discount department store for clothes. She pays on average $20-29 a dress and sometimes even less for a pair of summer sandals. She buys her grocery and household supplies at box-size stores and feels proud of paying a few dollars for a large basket of blueberries in the middle of fall. Often the family uses coupons to order pizza using "2 for 1" deals. Amy has her ears to the ground and knows when airline companies lower fares for cruises or overseas travel. Last winter she booked a 5-day cruise to Mexico for less than $500. She has solved the problem of gift giving to family and friends. Twice a year, on black Friday and 4th of July weekend, Amy buys dozens of gifts, wrapping paper, and cards that she anticipates will be needed for the coming months, all at discounted prices.

Katherine likes her cashmere sweaters that she bought a few years ago. Each year she wraps them and puts them away in a drawer with cedar blocks until next fall. She likes wool gabardine skirts for cold weather and linen for summer and updates her wardrobe with various sweaters and belts or scarves. She buys produce that is in season from local farmers' market, and often gives her friends gifts made from her kitchen. Last Christmas, she gave most of her friends bottles of extra virgin olive oil infused with either garlic or rosemary. She decorated the bottle with a sprig of fresh rosemary and a few colorful leaves along with a small hand made note tied to the bottle. Nieces and nephews got a coupon for "A day at the park with Katherine. Picnic lunch included."

Who gets your vote as being frugal?

Based on popular definition, Amy would be considered a frugal woman. After all, she is saving money by shopping at discount stores. Katherine wears cashmere sweaters. Isn't that extravagant?

For many, being frugal primarily means clipping coupons, hunting for bargain items on sale, or researching the Internet to find the best travel deal. While shopping smart is a great skill to have, its outcome is limited to saving money, not necessarily making us more content.

If we want to become more content through living frugally, we need to expand our definition of frugality beyond coupon clipping and the immediate monetary savings.

Taking a second look at Amy and Katherine changes the picture. Katherine buys high quality items and takes gentle care of them so her belongings last a long time. By shopping locally and buying produce that is in season, she is also ecologically more conscious. Amy may believe that the blueberries are cheap, but the cost of transporting blueberries from Mexico to her California table during fall is an environmental cost that remains hidden to her. From Katherine's gift giving style, it appears that she doesn't like to waste a lot of boxes and paper and creates gifts that are thoughtful and generate little waste—again conscious of the overall impact, not just to her personally but to the environment as well. Katherine is actually more frugal than Amy in the true sense of the word.

For Whom is This Chapter Written?

It is written for all of us. If you are wealthy and haven't had to worry about where the next jewelry comes from, this chapter will be a helpful reminder to be mindful of precious resources and reduce excess waste. On the other hand, if you have had serious financial set backs which have required you to watch every penny, this chapter might help you gain a different perspective on frugalness by focusing more on contentment rather than coupon clipping. Do allow yourself some enjoyable treats and remember that being frugal has nothing to do with deprivation.

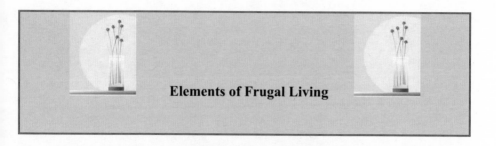

Elements of Frugal Living

Live within your means.

The concept of living within our means is similar to the message that we need to exercise or eat our vegetables. We know intellectually that it would benefit us, but few of us like to be reminded of it. At a deeper level, this concept brings us face-to-face with our limits as a human being. We are reminded that we don't have endless power, prestige or money, and someone is telling us, "No, you don't need to buy that." Most of us don't like to hear that. It's a blow to our omnipotence, so we go on spending as if there were no tomorrow.

People who chronically spend beyond their means are not content with what they have—they want more, and when they get it, they want even more. Greed becomes the #1 enemy of contentment. It has been said, "You can never get enough of what you don't need."

Here are a few tips to help get us started:

❖ **Differentiate between Wants and Needs.**
I look around the house and think that I need French patio doors for the living room, new bookshelves for the office, wooden blinds for the living room, and a new sink and tiles for the guest bathroom. Then I ask whether I *need* them or just want to have them.

- In fact, the sliding patio door works perfectly well, and most contractors prefer its design over a French door, especially during rainy season. The bookshelves in the office are not fancy, but they still have plenty of room for more books. Replacing the blinds and remodeling the bathroom would be purely cosmetic because there is nothing functionally wrong with either one.

- Does this mean that I would never allow myself to remodel my house? Of course not! The point is to ask *consciously* whether something is a need or a want, and then decide whether it is worthwhile to proceed. So far, I have waited on all five projects. If I change my mind, I will make sure that the funds are available to pay for them, and that high quality material is used that will last many years.

❖ **Pay cash or consider bypassing the purchase.** If you have traveled abroad to Europe or a developing country, you may have noticed that most people pay cash for every day purchases such as gas, groceries, restaurant food, and clothing. This is a good habit to develop especially for those who are accustomed to using a credit card for nearly every purchase.

- Paying cash makes the process of purchasing something more conscious—it's harder to part with cash than it is to hand over the credit card to the sales clerk.

- If you must use a credit card, be sure you can pay off the entire bill at the end of the month, or consider bypassing the purchase all together. Don't be seduced by the cash points or rewards the credit card companies offer for using their cards. The risk of becoming a credit card addict is far greater than the benefits the companies can ever offer you.

❖ **Save it before you see it!** It is true that the easiest way to save money is before it gets into your hands. Determine what a reasonable amount is for you and have it automatically deducted from your bank account into an investment account.

- To pay for travel or home improvement projects, it is always a good idea to have money saved ahead of time. You can estimate what is needed and have a monthly figure deducted automatically from your checking account into the *travel account* or *home improvement* account.

- Pay yourself a monthly sum for the house cleaning, yard work, and cooking that you do. Collect the money in an envelope and call it your slush fund. It is great fun to use it for whatever you desire—shopping, outing with your friends, or a special treat.

One of the enjoyable things about being frugal is becoming creative. We are *all* creative women—we just need to find a way to express that creativity. Some of us use words and writing; others use paint and drawing; while others use cooking and food to be creative. There are endless possibilities.

It is exciting to look around and discover a new use for something that you already have in the house or can acquire inexpensively. It becomes a fun game to discover how we can reduce waste at home.

Here are some ideas that can act as seeds of creativity so you can generate more of your own:

- ❖ Clean the inside of an empty coffee can that has a plastic lid. Cut a slit the size of a coin in the lid. Measure some fabric and glue it around the body of the can. You just made a piggy bank for a child.

- ❖ Line kitchen drawers with last year's calendar pages. It makes for a cheerful sight each time the drawer is opened.

- ❖ Tired of a framed mirror or a wooden picture frame? Give the frame a coat of paint and enjoy it for a while longer.

- ❖ Convert varying sizes of small terra cotta pots into candleholders by covering the bottom hole with a piece of tape and filling them with dry beans or rice. Place tall, dripless candles in them.

- ❖ Have unmatched socks? Put some dry lavender in a clean sock and tie the end. Place it in a drawer for a lovely scent.

- Wash off the labels from small glass spice jars; fill them with flowers and place a row of them on a party table. They make a statement as well as lovely hostess gifts.

- A mini ice cube tray placed in a vanity drawer holds dozens of earrings.

- Instead of letting the unused portion of a can of tomato paste go to waste, put table spoons on wax paper and place in the freezer until just frozen. Then transfer to a freezer container or bag, ready for future use.

- Wash garments as often as possible in cold water. It saves energy and makes your clothes last longer.

- Re-use plastic 1/2-cup applesauce containers in the kitchen for scooping out flour, sugar, cereals, etc.

- Place a wet paper towel in a reclosable sandwich bag and freeze it. Keep a few of them handy to use as a re-usable cold pack to soothe an aching body part.

- Heat a wet washcloth in the microwave until very hot. Wearing gloves, work fast and wipe kitchen cabinets. Rinse, heat the cloth again, and repeat. This method will dissolve grease quickly without using harsh chemical on the wood cabinets.

- Keep thin slices of lemons in a freezer bag. Drop one occasionally in the garbage disposal to deodorize.

Enjoy a simpler life.

Perhaps the best thing about being frugal is learning to enjoy a simpler lifestyle. It not only costs less, but also creates less stress, and is more eco-friendly. There is elegance to a simple life that no amount of wealth can buy.

How can we acquire the ability to enjoy a simple life? Getting older helps. As we get older, we tend to pay more attention to the essential things in life and fuss less about details that don't matter. Another factor is having experienced other cultures, humble lifestyles, or economic hardships. These experiences help us put in perspective our desires, and tame the long wish list that we carry. Sometimes a life-threatening illness or catastrophic event can jolt our priorities and awaken us to what is really important in life.

We don't have to wait until old age or foreign travel to begin the learning process. Here are some suggestions to consider:

Identify the source of stress or fuss in your life and take small steps to simplify. From morning to bedtime, what part of your routine seems too fussy and takes up a lot of your mental energy? Beauty routine? Cleaning and house chores? Commuting? Cooking and developing menus? Caring for the family? Weekend life? Entertaining?

Example #1 For Elizabeth, the answer was easy. It was her morning routine that she called fussy without hesitation. "I counted and found that I use 26 personal beauty products in the morning to get ready and four more in the evening," she said. This included dental and hair care products, skin care, face and eye make up, sunscreen, lotions and perfume. She often wasn't happy with her final finish because she wasn't sure if the colors she had picked suited the colors she was wearing.

Many of us can relate to this scenario: Drawer full of make up and we become overwhelmed. Elizabeth made an appointment with her hairdresser and specifically requested a low-maintenance hairstyle. Her wish was granted. This change cut in half both the time and the number of products she uses for her hair. She then scheduled a make up consultation at a department store and took all of her products with her. The make up artist was able to sift through and keep what suited Elizabeth's skin tone and taught her *one* basic routine that she could use regardless the color of clothes she was wearing. Elizabeth also learned to streamline her morning routine and use one product with multiple functions such as tinted skin lotion with sunscreen.

She now uses eight products in the morning, and four at night!

Example #2 Jennifer enjoys entertaining but she admits that she fusses about menu planning to a point where much of the fun is gone. We are not talking about having big parties, but weekly Sunday gatherings of her in-laws and adult children. She keeps switching back and forth between main dish choices and spends equal time on desserts.

Jennifer was willing to simplify this process by writing several compatible menus and rotating through them each week. For example, one Sunday night she fixed vegetarian lasagna with spinach and orange salad, garlic bread, and lemon bars for dessert. Another week, she had chicken with mushroom sauce, rice, two vegetables, rolls, and pie with ice cream for dessert. She had a shopping list ready for each menu and felt much more relaxed about the weekly family gatherings.

Cook meals at home. Not everyone's lifestyles permits them to cook meals at home, but it is something worth striving for, at least several days a week. Once you get into the rhythm of preparing most meals at home, you'll reap the benefits of healthier meals, lower cost, more family time, and greater joy.

Basic Kitchen Essentials:
- Have an assortment of dry herbs (dill, thyme, tarragon, cilantro, basil, parsley, bay leaf) and spices (cumin, cinnamon, coriander, curry, ginger, mustard, pepper flakes, etc) available
- Stock your pantry with various dry beans, rice, pasta, broth, nuts, dry fruits, tomato paste and sauce, balsamic vinegar, extra virgin olive oil, canola oil, dark sesame oil
- Salad spinner
- Steamer basket for vegetables
- Soup pot, small and large frying pan, couple of different sizes of pots
- Glass containers with plastic lids (freezer to microwave safe)

If you don't consider yourself to be a good cook, start easy. Try simple soups and supplement the meal with prepared pasta or other store bought side dishes. Little by little expand your repertoire.

Enjoy simple, unpretentious foods. Looking at recipes can be fun but I have little patience for recipes that call for fancy ingredients and want a little of this and a little of that. I end up buying a jar of a spice or herb and then never use it for another recipe. This is wasteful.

Over the years I have developed a taste for simple food that can be easily prepared with seasonal ingredients. I encourage you to use your senses (smell, touch, sight) to learn about cooking rather than wanting to follow an exact recipe. Unlike baking, cooking is forgiving and doesn't require exact measurements. Feel free to experiment with various proportions until you find one that suits your taste. Cooking cops will not arrest us if we add more carrot or less onion to a recipe. <u>Just have fun and release yourself from the bondage to exact measurements.</u>

Here are a few examples of simple, fuss-free foods that are nutritious, tasty, simple and inexpensive to prepare. I have included some measurements for those of you who are starting to cook and need to follow the recipe to the letter, but my hope is that as time passes, you let go of the measurements and let your eyes guide you in the process.

Peasant Potato soup

1) Over medium heat, melt 1-2 teaspoons of butter in a heavy saucepan. Add a large chopped white onion and 4-5 minced cloves of garlic. Add about 2 cups of chopped, unpeeled yellow potatoes and stir for a few minutes. Add a can and a half of chicken broth. Bring to a gentle simmer.

2) When the potatoes are done, using a potato masher, slightly mash the mixture while in the pot, leaving some chunks. Bring salt, pepper, and broth level to taste. A small of pinch of ginger powder is good too.

3) Ladle into soup plates and sprinkle some dill (preferably fresh) or other herbs such as tarragon. Mix and enjoy.

Pasta Mama This dish that can be supplemented with a fruit salad and served as a brunch dish, or a green salad and served as lunch or dinner.

1) For every two persons, break 3 large eggs in a bowl for. Add salt and some chopped fresh herbs (tarragon, chives, cilantro, basil or parsley) set aside.

2) In a non-stick frying pan, melt a small amount of butter and sauté 2 garlic clove per person without browning it. Set it on a plate.

3) Cook some angel hair or bow tie pasta in salted water and drain. Melt some butter in the frying pan and scramble the eggs. Work quickly and stir the pasta, garlic, and the eggs together. Add a handful of finely shredded Parmesan cheese, sprinkle more herbs and serve hot.

Cabbage vegetable soup

1) Over medium heat, melt 1-2 teaspoons of butter in a heavy saucepan. Add a chopped white onion and 3-4 crushed cloves of garlic. Add a cup of chopped, unpeeled potato and two large handfuls of finely shredded green cabbage. Stir until cabbage is wilted.

2) Add three cup of thinly sliced celery, a few chopped snap peas (optional), two cups of sliced carrots, a cup of rinsed frozen peas, and four cans of chicken broth. Bring to a gentle simmer. Add a teaspoon of dry dill. Adjust the salt, pepper and broth level to taste. Don't overcook. 8 Servings.

Lentil soup

1) Cook 2 cups of brown lentils in <u>un</u>salted water until al dente. Drain and set aside.

2) In a large soup pot, heat a tablespoon of canola oil or butter and add two chopped medium onions and 6-7 minced garlic cloves. Add 3 cups each of chopped celery and carrots. Stir for a couple of minutes.

3) Add a large can and 1-2 small cans of chicken broth and a cup of cooked lentils at a time until you think enough lentils have been added. Cover and simmer very gently.

Once the ingredients are done, there are two distinct different ways to season this hearty soup:

> ➤ Add 2-3 heaping tablespoons of tomato paste and salt to taste. <u>OR</u>
> ➤ Add all of these warm spices such as ground cumin, coriander, a dash of curry, cinnamon, and salt to taste. How much? It's up to your taste. Start easy!

Potato Frittata

1) Preheat the oven to 400 degrees. Thoroughly grease a 9x13 glass baking dish and add 1/4 cup canola oil to the bottom.
2) Sauté a large onion and some garlic in a tablespoon of oil.
3) Wash and cut up unpeeled potatoes into small cubes and boil them into salty water until almost done. Drain. Add some salt to the potatoes.
4) Break 8-9 eggs in a large bowl. Salt.
5) Heat the empty glass dish that has oil in it in the oven until hot.
6) Mix the eggs, potatoes, onion mixture and pour into the glass dish and bake until the top of the dish is browned.

7) Cool for 15 minutes. Cut into squares. Serve with a dollop of sour cream or plain Greek yogurt.

Fresh Pasta Marinara with Feta Cheese and Olives

1) Cut fresh organic tomatoes into large chunks and reserve the juice (one large per person).
2) Mince 2 garlic cloves per person and mildly sauté in oil. Set aside on a plate.
3) Cook white or whole-wheat pasta in salted water. Drain (do not rinse).
4) In a large frying pan over high heat, heat a tablespoon of corn or canola oil per person (not olive oil) until it smokes. Add the tomatoes (no juice) and keep the heat on very high for a few more minutes. Add the garlic and pasta. If the mixture needs more liquid, add some of the reserved juice.
5) Add several cubes of high quality feta cheese per person to the pasta mixture along with some drained kalamata olives.
6) Serve on plates and garnish with plenty of fresh basil.

Eggplant/lentil Spread

This a tasty dish that can be served as an appetizer with pita wedges and sour cream or as a summer lunch with small pitas, rings of sweet onion, lots of fresh herbs and a side green salad.

1) Cut 3-4 unpeeled Japanese eggplants into cubes and steam until tender.
2) Chop or thinly slice a large white or yellow onion and 6-7 large garlic cloves. Sauté in one tablespoon of canola or corn oil until soft and light brown.
3) Cook a cup of brown lentils in salted water until soft. Drain.
4) Add the eggplants to the onion mixture and with potato masher, mash the mixture until well blended.
5) Generously season with warm spices: cinnamon, coriander, ground cumin, a touch of curry. Salt and pepper to taste.
6) Start by adding a cup of cooked lentil at a time to the mixture and add more if needed. Continue to adjust the seasoning.

7) Serve at room temperature or slightly warm over small pita breads. Decorate with thinly sliced raw onion rings and fresh herbs.

Develop more gratitude.

If we make do with what we have, save more, waste less, and take pleasure in small things of life, then we will have become content. When asked, "What are you grateful for in life?" many say: "My family, my health, my job." They mention big things, which are of course worth gratitude. But this filters out many small things that happen every day that call for our attention and thanks. We live in a blessed country and we forget that many of our daily experiences would be considered unusual for people around the world. At this time, I have lived in the United States for over 31 years and here is a partial list of what I am grateful about nearly everyday:

- I turned on the faucet in the morning and running water came out just like every other morning.
- I flip the light switch and there is power.
- Every time I walk into a grocery, shelves are stocked with milk, bread, and other staples.
- If we get in an accident, an ambulance, fire truck and police arrive to help within minutes.
- I can buy any book that I want and my government won't jail me for reading it.
- The sales clerk was kind to the man who lacked change the other day.
- Mail carrier delivers mail without reading it or stealing the content.
- A little girl on a stroller said hi to me and showed me her doll.
- I had delicious blueberries this morning.
- My elderly friend is feeling better after spending a week in ICU.
- A teenager held the door open for an adult.

The more we look around, the more small things in life beckon us for gratitude.

Chapter 4 Value Your Time.

Your time is valuable and deserves to be invested wisely. Nurturing your family and caring for your career are also important goals. It is worth while to sit down and give some thought as to how best to structure your week so you could *optimize* your resources—this means maximizing your return and minimizing your stress.

*　　*　　*　　*

When Julia came to see me in my private practice, she seemed to have it all: wonderful children, a devoted husband, a nice job, a lovely home, good health, and many friends. Her chief complaints were irritability, low sex drive, fatigue, and lack of zest for life. "I want to be left alone for a long time," she said tearfully. What could be making her so unhappy? I wondered.

Julia was a 42-year old married woman who worked full-time as an office manager in a busy medical office. Her husband Kyle worked for a power company. He left the house early in the morning and was sometimes called to work unexpectedly at night. "I'm pretty much a single mother," she said half jokingly. They had 10-year old twins named Margaret and Madison. Kyle was a Boy Scout leader. Julia enjoyed teaching Sunday school at church and sometimes coached the girls' soccer team. They had no family in town.

Their home was typical of an upper middle class family and beautiful with a pool, landscaped yard, backyard BBQ with a tiled entertaining area, and newly remodeled kitchen, bathrooms and living room. Part of the reason the couple needed to work full-time and pay for the high mortgage was the numerous house-remodeling projects.

Julia was a busy woman. She woke up by 5:15 a.m.; prepared lunches; made breakfast; showered at 6:00; woke up her daughters; ate breakfast at 6:30. She left the house at 7:15 to drive her daughters to school so she could get to work by 8:00. She would take a 30-minute lunch, which allowed her to leave work at 4:30 and pick up her daughters, who were tired and cranky by then. On the drive home, sometimes she needed to pick up groceries. She would think about dinner, battle of the homework, paying bills, walking the dog, spending time with Kyle and crashing. She was glad that the math tutor was coming to their house instead of Julia driving an extra 15 minutes after school twice a week to her house. Saturdays were spent on shopping, laundry, and house cleaning until afternoon. Kyle helped only when Julia asked him to pitch in. He took care of the lawn and washed the cars every weekend, and helped the girls with their homework.

No wonder Julia was drained and exhausted. Millions of us wish we had more than 24 hours in a day to complete what needs to be done. We can easily relate to Julia's situation, but those of us who have more than two children, or live a less financially secure life, are under even more pressure by the demands of home and career.

What can be done to help?

For Julia the answer was not as simple as hiring a house-cleaner or ordering take-out a couple of nights a week. Kyle was on high blood pressure and cholesterol medications and the family wanted to be careful about meal preparation. Because they lived in a large house, paying someone to clean it weekly would have been costly, especially since they were trying to save money and pay off their mortgage.

In working with Julia, it soon became clear that her situation was a cultural epidemic: mothers feeling overwhelmed, and working mothers feeling even more exhausted and stretched. Much of Julia's progress consisted of learning how to organize her time--her life-- and spend it wisely as a precious commodity. She worked hard to implement many of the strategies suggested in this chapter, and within a few months calmness returned to her life and she felt more in control of her days. "I'm still doing the same things, but I'm not resentful and depressed anymore."

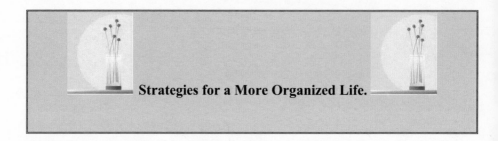

Strategies for a More Organized Life.

For much of this chapter, the assumption will be that you are a single, working mother and are not relying on any adult help around the house. If we can address this most challenging situation, then most other scenarios would be easier to cope with.

1. Befriend you calendar.

Productive and efficient people use their calendars as a personal assistant. Here are a few tips:

- o At the beginning of the year buy a wall calendar with large spaces and enter all birthdays or anniversaries in your calendar using one color pen. If you need to send a card to a friend, put "mail" 2-3 days before the event on your calendar. A wall calendar at home cannot be replaced by an electronic calendar.

- o Enter your appointments; including a phone number or address if you think you'll need them. This will save you time finding them when the appointment nears.

- o If an appointment is made months in advance for which you need to take something with you (e.g. document), note it on the calendar and remind yourself of the location of the item. For example, if your appointment is with the dentist and you need to take a form with you, mark "Take form in bottom desk drawer" on the calendar, next to the appointment.

o When you do a task that needs to be repeated periodically (e.g. fertilizing the yard), make a note 2-3 months after the event on the calendar by saying "3 months since fertilized the yard". If the yard looks like it needs fertilizer, do it then, otherwise, forward the reminder to the following month.

o When you change baking soda in the fridge or filter in the water pitcher, make a note a few months ahead on the calendar to repeat the task. Otherwise who'd remember to replace them regularly?

o Place reminders on the calendar with ample time for projects or events that require action on your part. For example, 2 weeks before a friend's wedding party, put "shop/mail wedding gift".

o Schedule your mammograms and annual physical exams on the same month as your birthday. They will be easier to remember.

2. Buy kitchen, bedroom, and office material that will help you stay organized.

Collecting gadgets cannot make a person organized but they can help if you get the right ones. Here are some tips:

o As you will see in the next section, having a few large plastic containers with lids is indispensable in the kitchen.

o Invest in an assortment of glass containers with plastic lids that are freezer to microwave safe.

o Buy a few tall, clear plastic storage containers for cereal, flour, sugar, rice, pasta, etc.

o If you can afford it, have an extra small freezer in the garage. It can save a working woman a lot of time during the week by storing already-prepared food.

o Buy plenty of colored hanging file and folders for your desk for various topics. Colored markers help. Tag your name on your pens or else everyone else in your family will walk away with them and your desk remain disorganized.

3. Plan ahead.

o Stock up on non-perishables. Here is a rule of thumb: If it doesn't need to be refrigerated, it doesn't need to be purchased more than twice a year (bananas and onions excluded!). This list includes toiletry, detergent, canned goods, paper products, stamps, pantry items, light bulbs, batteries, office products, lawn and garden products, cleaning products, school supplies, vitamins and over-the-counter products, greeting cards, gift-wrap and a host of other things that make the list grow too long. The point is that your precious time need not be spent running to the store for cotton balls or a can of tomato paste.

o When you purchase an item that needs future parts to function (e.g. vacuum cleaner bags, light bulbs for a lamp, butane refills for BBQ, etc.), buy a few extra refill or parts at the time of purchase. It will save you time later, and you may even be told that they don't make that item anymore.

- Make routine doctor and hair appointments months in advance. You'll have more choices.

4. Save time on your chores.

- Do many of your errands when there is less traffic on the road or in the store (e.g. early morning or weekend). For instance, for the twice-a-year bulk shopping, it is worth it to get to the store early in the morning with a detailed shopping list. This is also true for weekly tasks such as getting gas for the car or money from the bank.

- Use technology to your advantage. Pay bills on-line. It not only saves time and money, but also allows you to monitor your accounts thus reducing possible fraud.

- Before making a trip to a store to purchase a special item, call to see if they have it in stock. Even ask in what aisle it is.

- When purchasing an item that was packaged at the factory (e.g. electronics, household items), open and inspect it at the store. It'll save you three trips to take it home and return it should it turn out to be damaged or incomplete.

- When you look up a number in the phone book, mark it with a bright pen. You'll be surprised how many times you'll refer to it again, only this time effortlessly. I even write down in the phone book the extension I need to press next time I call.

- Always keep a few stamps and an extra $20 bill tucked away in a small pocket of you your wallet. It'll save time when you are in need.

- o Until they make dryers that don't eat socks, put your children's socks in a laundry mesh when doing laundry. It saves you time looking for lost pairs in the dryer.

5. Act, file, or shred.

Set aside a few minutes a day to go through the daily mail, and decide right away whether something needs to be responded to, or shredded. Don't read and put it away only to come back another day to read and put it away again. That's a waste of time.

6. Work efficiently in the kitchen.

Preparation of meals is a daily event that can siphon a lot of time from a working woman's schedule. I have found the following strategies have completely changed my time commitment in the kitchen and brought me enormous relief—even though I love to cook.

Cooking is an enjoyable act but many working women are conflicted about cooking from scratch because they simply do not have the time to prepare healthier meals when they get home. It is a repetitive task and can become overwhelming unless we have some strategies in place. Remember, we are assuming that you are a working single mother, and are cooking most meals at home. Here are some suggestions:

- o Plan the weekly dinner menu and shop for everything you need early Saturday morning. Let's use the following sample menu. It may not be what you serve your family, but it can illustrate our main points.

<u>Saturday</u>	BBQ, Rice, Salad with lots of Vegetables
<u>Sunday</u>	Lasagna, Salad, Green Vegetable
<u>Monday</u>	Stir-fry (meat or tofu), Rice
<u>Tuesday</u>	Meat balls, sweet potato oven fries, Veggies
<u>Wednesday</u>	Soup, frozen Quiche*
<u>Thursday</u>	Spaghetti w/ meat sauce, fresh vegetables, garlic bread
<u>Friday</u>	Pizza*, Soup

* Can be store bought

There are four secrets in the menu above.

<u>First</u> is that the menu puts the dinners that require greater preparation on weekends, and weeknight dinners require little cooking. When you cook rice for the weekend meal, save and freeze some for Monday.

<u>Second</u> is that salad is incorporated earlier in the week and then we have vegetables or soup for the rest of the week. That's because salad ingredients are more perishable and we are assuming that you are only making one trip to the store.

<u>Third</u>, the dinner for our busiest night of the week (Wednesday) is very simple and already prepared.

<u>Fourth</u>, this menu is planned so that as you prepare one dish (Lasagna), the ingredient (meat) can be used for the spaghetti sauce and meatballs as well. "Foods of a feather cook together."

*　　*　　*　　*

o   Spend an hour, or even less, washing and trimming the salad material and vegetables. Dry the salad using a salad spinner and store the lettuce or other green leafy salad ingredients in the rectangle containers you have, <u>placing</u>

61

<u>paper towels in between the layers</u>. This will absorb extra moisture and keep your salad fresh for days. Be sure you place a paper towel just below the lid.

- o Do the same with vegetables. Wash the carrots with a vegetable brush; dry and place in a container; trim the celery, cauliflower, etc. Make sure you place paper towels over and in between before storage. The paper towels are not being wasted because you can always re-use them later. Spending an hour a week prepping the vegetables ensures that you have the ingredients for dinner all week. You can even chop the stir-fry veggies for Monday and store them in a separate container.

- o Now start cooking. The key to saving time in the kitchen is to cook similar items at once and start by the "cleanest" dish first. What does that mean? It means make a pot of vegetable soup and a pot of lentil (or minestrone) soup simultaneously. The basic ingredients are the same (onions, garlic, celery, carrots); you just add different beans to the two soups later. When you make two soups at once, you will have variety within a week, and will be able to take some for lunch. Store and freeze the soups in glass containers with plastic lids.

- o Next, without washing anything, move on to the preparation of the meat. That's what I meant by starting with the cleanest dish first. It cuts down on your dishwashing. Shape and cook the meatballs, meat sauce for the spaghetti, and the lasagna sauce. Store appropriate portions in re-closable freezer bags or glass containers. Hurray! You spend a couple of hours cooking and are done for the week!

- o Let's assume it's Monday. Before leaving home, take out some rice, meatballs (or shrimp) from freezer and let them defrost in the fridge. When you get home, the vegetables are ready; rice and meat (or tofu) are in the fridge. All you need to do is open a bottle of sauce and stir-fry. Always make enough dinner so you can take some for lunch the next day.

o   Another time-saving tip is that as you prepare fruit for dessert, cut up some for next day lunches and next day's after school snacks or dessert. The killer in the kitchen is the clean up. Minimize it by bundling the chores. Have a large pan of hot soapy water in the sink. Put in things after using and washing is easy.

o   Other preparations you can make in advance are cooking beans. They are nutritious, inexpensive and wonderful additions to salads, soups, rice, and pasta. Cook a couple of different types of dry beans separately at a time (e.g. lentils, black eyed peas, black beans, etc.); measure what you need and store them in reclosable sandwich or snack bags. Place the bags in a heavier freezer bag. This saves you space in the freezer as well as money by using fewer freezer bags.

o   You can also chop fresh herbs; portion for future use, and freeze them in freezer-safe containers. It is very convenient to have chopped herbs available when cooking soups, stir fries, omelets, etc.

o   If your family eats meat, cut up chicken or beef into stir-fry pieces; portion and place them in reclosable sandwich bags. Place the bags in a heavier freezer bag. When you leave the house in the morning, place a bag in the fridge. By evening, the meat is ready to be rinsed and pat dried. It will cook within minutes on high heat. You can have dozens of such bags in your freezer for convenience.

o   I enjoy baking and like to shape cookie dough into little balls and freeze them in freezer bags. When the need arises, I take out as many as needed and bake them fresh. They also make a wonderful gift for someone who doesn't bake but enjoys eating!

*   *   *   *

Now let's get wise and ask for help around the house. I believe that anyone older than 12-13 is fully capable of cooking a meal for a family. This doesn't have to be a gourmet meal, but the teens have to be able to pull it off by themselves in case you are not available.

- o If you have teens in this age range or older, let them pick a simple meal and practice cooking it with them once a month until they master it.

- o Children as young as 4 can pack a healthy lunch if shown how. I had told my daughter she could pick one item from each of the three drawers in the fridge when she was in preschool. <u>Drawer one</u> had dairy items (string cheese, little containers of yogurt, cheese squares). <u>Drawer two</u> had kid-friendly fruit such as small apples, easy-to-peel tangerines, applesauce, packages of prunes, fruit leather, and small boxes of 100% orange juice. <u>Drawer three</u> had baby carrots, celery with peanut butter, packages of trail mix, small granola bars, and I occasionally slipped in a treat such as a chocolate bar which immediately was selected!

- o Your evenings are best spent helping your children, working out, making lunches for the next day, and recharging. As much as you can, try to prepare meals on weekends so you don't stress yourself every night in the kitchen, <u>and</u> help your family become self-sufficient so they can pitch in.

Chapter 5   Don't Get Mad at the Acorn!

Which of the following scenarios annoy you or hurt your feelings?

a) ___You are in the express check out counter at the grocery store and the person in front of you has many items to check out including some return items.

b) ___Receptionist has put you on hold to enjoy elevator music.

c) ___People have often treated your smarter sibling more favorably.

d) ___You keep running into red lights in traffic.

e) ___Your dog has fleas.

f) ___Your in-laws do not show the same level of affection to your children as your parents.

g) ___Your housemate lets dishes pile up in the sink for days before washing them.

h) ___Strong wind knocks down the flowerpot and breaks it.

i) ___Your boyfriend seems less interested in you now that you've dating for a year.

j) ___The appliance repairman shows up two hours later than the scheduled time.

k) ___Your child throws a tantrum and embarrasses you in public.

l) ___Your friend keeps answering her cell phone while you are having lunch together.

m) ___You notice that as you get older, men do not pay as much attention to you as they once did.

n) ___Your check bounced.

o) ___Your Thanksgiving flight is cancelled due to weather and you are stuck at the airport.

p) ___Once again the drier ate a few socks during the wash and you ended up with mismatched pairs.

If you have checked more than six of these, then this chapter is for you.

*　　*　　*

A couple of years ago, I had an experience that changed the way I react to annoying happenings in life. One summer evening I was standing in line to get cash from an ATM. I could hear a few kids play in the parking lot. It was a breezy evening. Just as I approached the window, a small object hit my head. I immediately became mad at the kids who had thrown it at me. I said to myself that as soon as I received my withdrawal slip, I was going up to walk up to those children and give them a piece of my mind. Then something hit the top of my right shoulder. I looked up. Sure enough, there was a big tree next to the ATM dropping acorns. My anger vanished. I was embarrassed at how quickly I had judged the children, and how needlessly I had taken the incident personally. Now that the acorn was the identified perpetrator, what was there for me to be angry at? The tree? The wind? The acorn? I couldn't be mad at them; they weren't people. They had no will.

What Does an Acorn Have to do With Daily Life?

The arithmetic seems simple. When people do something that hurts or irritates you, shouldn't they be held accountable for their actions? Building on this logic, we give ourselves permission to get mad at them for their inconsiderate behavior.

And while we are at it, we hold on to the grudge for a long time and keep building on it. Now we're even. Sound familiar?

Undoubtedly many of us do just that and get mad several times a day over the types of things that I have outlined above. Some of you can relate to the acorn story and say: "Of course I see that you can't get mad at the dog with fleas because it's an animal and has no control over its environment". But it may be less obvious to see how the other examples relate to the story. For example, when we are put on hold on the phone for a long time, of course it's the company's fault for not hiring enough customer service staff. What about when our mate loses interest in us? There is no acorn here, right?

Acorns Fall Everywhere!

We can justify our anger and ruin what could be a perfectly ordinary day. This anger can only have toxic consequences for our health and the longevity of our relationships.

In fact every example listed above is actually another silly acorn falling on our shoulder.

First of all, feeling angry is not always a bad thing. Sometimes we need to be outraged at the senseless cruelty that we witness, but anger is only helpful if we follow it with constructive action and energetic goodwill. Unfortunately, most of the time our anger isn't channeled constructively and ends up tearing at the fabric of peace. Anger siphons away helpful energy from us; resentment drags us down.

In the Introduction, I mentioned that content women seem to have some energy left for them at the end of the day. They seem to have found a way to stop the draining and not let precious energy go to waste by getting angry frequently. What kinds of things are these women releasing?

If you go back and read the list at the beginning of this chapter, try to spot a few obvious examples that are typical acorn scenarios (The drier eating the socks; wind breaking the flower pot, etc.) With practice, you can recognize many more acorn situations in your daily life and not react to them as before. (Perhaps *acorn* has already entered our vocabulary in a new way!)

Now let's work on some strategies for the less obvious examples on the list.

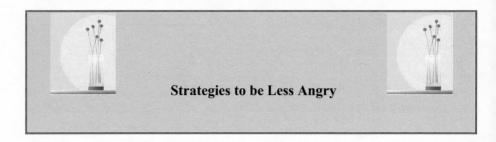

Strategies to be Less Angry

Strategy #1: Adjust your expectations.

We can expect that people should arrive on time and flights should depart on schedule. But if we do that, we are only setting ourselves up for frustration when the outcome doesn't match our rosy expectation. The bigger the gap between our <u>expectations</u> and an <u>outcome</u>, the more room will be available for anger to fill. Try and close this gap. Next time the wind blows leaves on your freshly raked lawn and you get annoyed, immediately challenge your thinking and say this aloud to yourself: "Are you expecting no wind in this world? Wind happens! Rake the lawn and move on. Enjoy the day."

General expectations about people or life can lead to unnecessary disappointment, but so can expectations about temporary events. Let's say that you have planned a weekend getaway with a special friend. Some of us fantasize so much about what we are going to do during this romantic time that we cash in early on the weekend. By the time the trip comes to an end, we feel a let down and a sense of disappointment. "It wasn't as good as I had hoped." Now, it's all right to plan broadly the kind of activities you are going to do with your friend (hiking, eating out, etc.), but resist the temptation to build up any expectation, high or low, until you are there and are experiencing the moment. Life doesn't need many rehearsals.

Does this mean that we should lower our expectations and settle for a mediocre job or relationship just so we don't get disappointed in life? No! We need to adjust the expectations to match reality for things over which we have little or no control. When you *can* control how well you do at work or another task, then set reasonable expectations for yourself and reap the benefits.

Strategy #2: Accept what is.

We only create anger for ourselves, and hurt for others, when we try to force them to do things our way. Take an example from everyday life at home:

Michelle is a tidy person and likes to keep the shared walk-in closet neat and organized. She hangs her clothes right away and puts her shoes where they belong. Her husband, Bruce, throws the towels on the rack. He often aims for the hamper, but the gym clothes often miss their mark.

Michelle believes that she is right and the towels should be folded. Bruce feels picked on. This is a familiar scenario. They can argue over this and other little idiosyncrasies all day, but the point is that Michelle is who she is and Bruce is who he is. Like the left and the right hands, they each have an equal right to exist and function according to their nature. Michelle probably was aware of this difference before marrying Bruce. If she was, then she can either ask him kindly to accommodate her preference for neatness, or fold the towels herself, *without* judgment, or resentment. Contrary to popular practice, this issue doesn't need marriage counseling or endless analysis and communication about why each person is this way. This is an acorn falling on a shoulder.

Strategy #3: Accept what is--even if it is painful.

We are now going to turn up the heat a little bit and talk about a few unpleasant things in life such as finding out our parent is developing dementia; a relationship just ended and left us with a broken heart; a good friend is diagnosed with stomach cancer; our grandchild has got into drugs; the family pet died. The list goes on.

Most of us tend to react to such news with dismay, sadness, and some anger at the universe. Some of us may feel victimized and ask "Why me?" Of course we get sad when a friend has cancer, or when a lover leaves. We are human and have feelings. It would be unreasonable to expect that we go on with life as if nothing has happened. What gets us in trouble is not the fact that we experience a period of sadness or disbelief upon hearing such news, but that we continue to battle with it as if what has happened is terrible, wrong, and should never have happened in the first place. We try to stop it; we join support groups to talk to others about it, and we run ourselves down vowing to fight it. Meanwhile, the anger grows quietly underneath. We may have an assumption of what life ought to be like, and when such events happen, then we think something has gone awry with our life.

I am not suggesting for a moment that we should roll over and do nothing to take care of our feelings when we are faced with a challenge. What I am saying is that if we learn to cope with the event *without* assuming that what has occurred should not have happened, then we can prevent a lot of our energy from going to waste.

There is a big difference between expecting a life without illness, hardship, or loss versus accepting the fact that these are indeed ingredients of life—not ingredients of an *unfortunate* life—but of life. Friends get sick; people die; floods and fires destroy homes; lovers quit. These are undeniable facts of life just like getting wet when we go out in the rain or watching a glass break when we drop it.

Women who understand this principle save a great deal of their precious energy from going to waste. Their reaction to the event is proportioned and tamed. These women are

70

not cold and insensitive; they have learned not to go head to head with the hard facts of life and fight laws of nature. Instead, they use their conserved energy constructively to help themselves and others, thus bypassing the unnecessary pain and anger.

Strategy #4: Stop trying to fix your mate.

Many women who heard the title of my book as I was writing it asked me what the six secrets were. They were hoping I'd devote a long chapter on how to improve their intimate relationships with spouses or boyfriends, which of course I have not done.

Women who spend a lot of time and energy trying to improve their intimate relationship may end up feeling more frustrated and resentful than women who invest that energy in themselves. Many women have essentially become another mother for their mates: they watch what he eats, police his workouts, chastise him if he doesn't smile in family pictures, and tuck his shirt in public. This is embarrassing and chokes off romance.

The paradox is that, on one hand we mother our mates inappropriately, and on the other hand, we remain little girls expecting them to protect us and cover up our insecurities. We will be a lot more content if we pursue our own wellness, monitor our own food, clothing, and conduct, and then watch our mates grow closer to us in the space that has been created in the relationship.

Strategy #5: Understand the evolutionary force behind our relationships.

How can the acorn story be used to help us with things such as:

- ❖ When our mate cheats on us.
- ❖ When we no longer feel attracted to the same person whom we thought was our soul mate.
- ❖ When in-laws are less effusive toward your children than your parents, etc.

I have to admit it has taken me a long time to write this section of the chapter because I suspected that I might alienate many readers at this point if I don't explain this principle clearly.

Our definition of what a healthy, romantic relationship or marriage ought to be has undergone major changes in the last sixty years as the society has witnessed exponential growth in the number of women who join the workforce, as well as the growth of their earning power. To this, add enormous technological and scientific changes that influence our lives and how we relate to each other.

But the time frame during which these changes have happened is tiny and insignificant compared to the hundreds of thousands of years that it has taken for our human species to evolve. In other words, just because *we* think that we should be treated equally in society regardless of our appearance, it doesn't mean that evolution has hardwired us to treat each other equally. In fact, it has programmed us to do the opposite: to favor those who look healthier and more attractive because they are the ones with the higher odds of attracting social attention and thus better survival.

Some of you may not like what I am about to say next, but bear with me. We are approaching really hot coals here! We women feel deeply hurt if our mate shows interest in other women or has an affair. Again, we are human and hardwired to feel jealous. Now, if we look at it strictly from evolution's point of view, here is how the picture looks: A man's job is basically done after ejaculation. Done. Finished. Nature wants him to move on and spread his sperm to propagate the species. Meanwhile, *we* want him to stay with us, paint the nursery, compliment us on our cooking, help the kids with homework, coach the soccer the team, and adore us for the next thirty years.

These are completely different agendas that nature has produced for men and women. Obviously they clash in today's society in which we have *recently* developed the belief that we should stay forever faithful to each other. Believe me, I am not advocating promiscuity here. What I am saying is that we create a great deal of hurt and anger for ourselves when we don't understand evolution's trigger points in us. We are trying to impose the modern social and romantic model on life, and genes don't give a hoot about that.

So where do we go from here?

Just because nature has hardwired us to act a certain way, it doesn't mean that we are doomed to behave like robots.   We all have experienced moments when we were so angry that we almost could have hit someone, but we showed restraint and didn't. What stopped us? We may have reflected a few seconds about the consequences of our action and decided not to act on our reflex or primitive brain.

Using the same logic, just because we are hard wired to be attracted to healthier and younger men or women, it doesn't mean that we should always follow this evolutionary rule like sheep. Though I might feel the initial reflex, I can then have a little talk with myself and move from a <u>reflexive</u> to a <u>reflective</u> position.

The same kind of logic applies to a man who feels compelled by nature to spread his genes to many women. He too can own the initial reflex, but move into the reflective position and realize the value and warmth of a long-term relationship with a stable mate and the growth that it can bring.

The main point is this: Try not to fight with nature by ignoring evolution's agenda. Be conscious of it in daily relationships, but move beyond it using the reflective part of your. That's what content women seem to have learned to do.

Women who live with their best friend are deeply content.

A few years ago I was at the Cathedral of Notre Dame in Paris. My cousin said that I could buy a candle and make a wish. "The custom is that when the wish comes true, you return and light the second candle," she explained. I didn't know what to wish for, nor did I want to waste my wish on something whimsical. I sat on a bench and thought of what was important in my life. What came to my mind was: "May I know when my best friend is in my life." Several years passed. Every once in a while I would open the drawer of my nightstand and wonder whether my wish had come true. How would I know if it had?

One day, as I was talking to a wise, elderly friend about my life and daily routine, he said: "It sounds like you are your best friend, Azarm." It was at that moment that I realized the profound wish that I had made at Notre Dame had come true.

*   *   *   *

I once heard a woman say on a talk show that she doesn't invite people over to her house as often as she would like because she has to clean her living room, change the tablecloth, clean the bathroom, and serve food in nicer dishes. "I live alone so it doesn't matter what I do when I am by myself."

Her statement made an impression on me. I started noticing a widespread use of a double standard among many women in the sense that they treat others differently than themselves. The statement I just made wouldn't surprise psychologists; they have known for a long time that people act differently in a social setting than in private. We know that we pick our nose and play with our toes when we are home alone, but we tend not to do that in front of company. The point here is that we clean the house for company, but tolerate dirty floors for ourselves. Why do we treat others nicer?

Do You Treat Your Friends Better Than You Treat Yourself?

If you said "no", you'd be in a small minority. Not only do many women treat their friends better than themselves, they are usually their own worst enemies. They criticize their bodies mercilessly and constantly second guess the decisions they make. They are quick to take responsibility for things that have gone wrong when it wasn't their fault; they say, "I'm sorry" when they really ought to say "Your turn to apologize", and they often think that what they have done is not good enough. With this kind of self-abuse, who needs an enemy?

How Do We Treat Our Best Friend?

Chances are we generously compliment our best friend (Let's assume it's a she); offer to help her when she is overwhelmed; we support her when she is sad and try not to make her feel more guilty if she has made a mistake; we celebrate her special occasions and give her gifts; we forgive her for the sake of our friendship; we share recipes and tips; we try to have fun with her; we make time for her; listen to her, and do our best to boost her self-esteem.

What Does it Meant to Live With Your Best Friend?

It is clear we are not talking about moving in with your best friend, or marrying your best friend. The message of this chapter is to encourage you to treat yourself like a best friend so you gradually become kinder to yourself. Think of the wonderful example you'll be setting for your family, especially your daughters.

Eleven Things You Can do to Become Your Own Best Friend

1. Surround Yourself with Beauty

We may have different tastes, but we respond to a beautiful surrounding with positive emotions. Find what is aesthetically pleasing to you and make an effort to gradually incorporate that into your surroundings. Here are some suggestions:

- A typical home is too cluttered. Even people who are used to clutter say that once the clutter is gone, they find themselves calmer and able to think more clearly. Does the fridge need to be covered with papers and magnets? Do bills have to sit on the kitchen counter? Surprise yourself by de-cluttering your home and discovering its hidden beauty. You'll have fewer knick-knacks to dust.

- Creating beauty does not have to cost money. Use a scarf or shawl as a tablecloth; stack a set of decorative books on a table and place a candle or picture frame on top; coordinated picture frames make a lovely table arrangement; find new uses for a pretty plate or an old vase; A bowl of red apples in a wooden dish is a stunning centerpiece, so is a bowl of green apples in a colorful dish; use and re-use what you have!

- Some women postpone beauty until their children are grown. They are afraid children will break things. Who can forget the 18-month old who pulls the tablecloth to the floor along with everything that's on it? Yes, it is sensible to take precaution to a point, but to ban beautiful things only postpones the child's learning.

Here's why: A child who eats from a plastic plate and drinks from a sippy cup until the age of five doesn't learn what breakable means. Let her experience what it feels like when she breaks a dish. Help her sweep it up. Next time she'll walk more carefully to the kitchen and hold her glass with more care. Let's stop cushioning the landings for our children.

- Be daring in the use of wall color. It is the least expensive way to decorate a room. You'll be surprised how color affects your mood. A cheerful lemon yellow or a warm sand color can both be beautiful for the right room. If you don't want to paint the entire room, paint one wall with an accent color and enjoy the effect.

- Keep your bedroom as your sanctuary, especially if you have children. Some couples' bedrooms look like another playroom and are filled with toys and children's books. A couple needs adult space and access to a beautiful, romantic place for retreat. Children will learn to respect that and will actually feel better about the strength of your bond.

- Many women treat their home as their nest. They are proud of it; and like it neat and beautiful but complain that their spouses or children mess it up. You can help by providing a basket for the newspapers, or a shoe rack, but they need to keep the rest of the mess in the children's room or garage. The living room is community property and one person doesn't have the right to trash it.

- Nourish all of your senses, not just the eyes. As recent studies show, lovely music or a gently scented lotion can go a long way in soothing you on a stressful day. Why not light a candle at dinner? If your teenager makes fun of you, smile back and say: "This one is for me."

- Try to have fresh flowers at home and your office. It does miracles for your mood. If you are reluctant to pay for it at first, here is an indirect way you can fund this: Save the change and $1 dollar bills from you wallet in a jar, and use that to buy yourself flowers. That'll be your "flowers piggy bank."

- If you pack a lunch to work, make sure you have a nice plate and utensils in your office as well as a few nice napkins. Pack your lunch in a beautiful and appetizing way, just as you would if you were sharing it with an officemate.

2. Learn to Soothe Yourself

Learning to soothe ourselves is a major step toward befriending ourselves. Many of us only know how to deal with difficult emotions by overeating, excessively worrying, or engaging in other self-defeating behaviors. The result is not effective because we end up feeling worse. You may want to try some of the following ideas next time something bothers you. Keep in mind that one idea may not work in all situations. Therefore it is desirable to have multiple skills in your repertoire.

- Decide ahead of time that you are no longer going to make matters worse when feeling upset by eating cookies or ice cream from the container. You wouldn't shove cookies down your best friend's mouth if she were upset. Would you? Let's not do that to ourselves either.

- Validate that something is bothering you, and if you can, label the feeling. "I'm mad, angry, scared, jealous, etc." Next, gauge whether this is a chronic, recurring issue (e.g. feeling lonely, interpersonal conflict at work), or a temporary one (e.g. bad traffic, dinner is not ready, PMS).

  If it is <u>temporary</u>, you need to buy some time until the crisis passes. Wash your face, take deep breaths, smell a candle scented with lavender, and tell yourself that "things aren't working out the way you had hoped tonight, but you are not going to let that ruin the rest of your evening."

  If the issue is <u>chronic</u>, nip it in the bud by saying: "I have felt this way before, and wasn't able to solve it just by thinking about it. I am not going to repeat that tonight." Then go on to your First Aid Kit (below). But keep in mind that you need to work on a solution sooner or later.

- Create an <u>Emotional First-Aid Kit.</u> Every home has a First-Aid Kit for physical wounds. You can create one for when your heart is aching. Start with a basket or a large, decorative box. Put a few special items that make you feel warm and fuzzy. For instance, when I created my kit a few years ago, I put the first tiny pair of shoes my daughter wore, some lovely letters from dear friends, a journal, a few pictures, a lively dance CD (nothing sad to listen to at this point), a couple of Mother's Day gifts that my daughter made for me at primary school, etc. Every once in a while, I changed the selection of contents to keep it fresh.

Today, I have a secretary's desk in my bedroom that is my *sanctuary*. There is a small lamp on it along with a lavender-scented candle, a few hand-painted rocks, couple of pictures that melt my heart, a leather journal, a beautiful assortment of stationery, and a kind note that I may have received lately in the mail. Each time I retreat to this corner, it soothes me, wraps me with love, and makes me want to go on stronger than before. That's self-soothing.

3. Protect Yourself from Toxic Emotions

We all have days when we simply cannot shake off our sadness, anger, loneliness, resentment, envy, and other disturbing emotions. Many relationships are ruined as a result of our inability to control such emotions and keep things in perspective. I have two personal thoughts to share about this important issue.

- One spring afternoon I left the house for my daily walk. It was raining so I took an umbrella. At the end of the walk, I realized that it was no longer raining. In fact, there was a rainbow in the sky and the birds were singing. By holding the umbrella over my head for a long time and looking down at the pavement, I had missed a lot of beauty along the way. Immediately, I realized that this is similar to what we do with our toxic emotions; we hang on to them, carry them with us for too long when we no longer need to, long after the event is over. We stay angry an hour, two days, ten years after a conversation has taken place just as I held on to the useless umbrella for half of my walk.

- Do you remember the witch-like figures in fairy tales who were mean to children, or the nasty stepmother who prevented Cinderella from going to the ball? We are not children anymore, but many of us still carry the mean and critical voice of a witch within us. It tells us "You're fat; If you were prettier, your husband wouldn't have had that affair; Can't you do anything right? You're getting old; You've messed up your children, etc."

These thoughts come at us relentlessly and we feel overwhelmed. Unfortunately, we feel we cannot do anything about them. Of course we can! What would you do if a person was standing in front of you and putting you down and constantly criticizing you? I hope you'd say: "You have no right to speak to me that way. Go away." You need to do the same thing with these unkind, toxic thoughts and emotions. Try saying any of the following in a *calm* way:

"Go away. I was doing fine without you."
"Here you are again. I am not going to listen to you."
"Go back to where you came from."

You can push back on these thoughts and shield yourself from them. You may have to do this a dozen times a day, but eventually the volume goes down, although it might never go away completely.

I am using the *witch* analogy to make a point here, but we can use any vocabulary—call the critical voices a decrease in Serotonin level in the brain or anything else that you like. It is harder to talk back to a neurotransmitter for me than visualize putting a *witch* in her place!

---

4. Be Selective About People with Whom You Socialize

We usually can't choose our co-workers, but we can be selective about whom we see *after* work.

- It is important to remember that social contacts that are not work related are primarily optional. You have a say in the frequency and the depth of a friendship. Sometimes much unhappiness results from friendships, as had happened between one of my clients and her friend. I inquired about the nature of their relationship; it turns out my client didn't even enjoy socializing with this friend but couldn't quite give herself permission to quit.

- There may be a relative who is hard to get along with. You just need to minimize your contact to a point where you can tolerate him/her without damaging your relationship permanently. This means declining some social functions, arriving late and leaving early to other engagements, etc.

5. Guard Your Sleep

Are you surprised that this topic made it to the top 10 list? Lack of rest is a contributing factor to many of the problems women face, including irritability, anxiety, fatigue, weight gain and depression.

- The title of this section asks you to "Guard" your sleep, implying that other factors can infringe upon your sleep and it is your responsibility to guard it as a precious commodity. Family demands, social obligations, unfinished chores, all will tempt you to stay up late. What will you say? "It's time for me to rest." Soon others will get the message that you are off limit at that time.

- Some women go to bed after everyone else and get up first in their household because that's the only way they get some quiet time. They are solving one problem by creating another. Depending on how old your children are, you can expect that they be in their rooms by a certain time because "the house is going to sleep." As they get older, it is harder to keep this rule, but you can retire to your room and relax as long as your teens know how to put the house to sleep. Remember, you can't be the CEO 24 hours a day, therefore you need to trust them.

- Count 7-8 hours backwards from the time you need to wake up in the morning and gradually work toward going to bed at that time in the evening. Dim the lights; play softer music; journal; avoid television in your bedroom; turn off the telephone ringer; read a soothing passage, and write down any lingering worries on a note pad so you don't have to carry them into your sleep.

6. Speak Kindly to Yourself

Thank heavens we can't hear our thoughts, otherwise we might be aghast at how we speak to ourselves. We may not hear the thoughts, but eventually we can feel the *feelings* that are born of the thoughts. When a client tells me that she has been feeling bad about herself, it turns out that many of her thoughts have had a particular tone. This is also true with feelings of depression, envy, or anxiety.

- As you get dressed or put make-up on, speak to yourself as if you are talking to your good friend. Instead of thinking how drab you look, or noticing the crow's feet around your eyes, smile and say: "THIS is my color!" or "I look good in this accessory today!", or "Hello, Gorgeous!"

- When you make a mistake in the kitchen, don't say: "That was dumb." Your children will copy you like parrots. Are you sure you want them to call themselves dumb? Say: "Oops, let's try again." Never say: "I'm so stupid."

- No one has the right to speak unkindly to you, including you!

7. Be the Guest at the Table Every Time

This suggestion becomes especially relevant if you live alone because many single people drift into a lifestyle of "it's-just-me-so-who-cares?"

- Treating yourself with respect won't make you arrogant. It would if you treated yourself special and everyone else worse; I am not suggesting that you do that. Treat yourself as you would treat your other guests, this way everyone wins.

- Eating is one of the most pleasurable experiences of life, and it is unfortunate that we have hurried the cooking and eating process to a point of insanity. Perhaps you can help change that one meal at a time in your kitchen.

- Set a nice table with a candle, a small vase with a single flower. Plates and silverware don't have to match; they just need to look aesthetically appealing to you. Trust your taste. Arrange the food in palatable way on a plate. Be creative:
    - ♣ A large wine glass can be a lovely container for fruit salad mixed with layers of yogurt.
    - ♣ Put a few cube of cheese and olive on toothpicks.
    - ♣ Make a fruit kabob on a skewer and serve it on a plate.
    - ♣ If you prepared the meal for others, preside at your table and take satisfaction in what you have done and in the enjoyment others take from your food.

The possibilities are endless. You may be wondering why go through all this trouble just for yourself? That's the whole point. You do it for yourself. You matter.

8. Listen to Your Body

If your best friend says she has a migraine and is not feeling well, would you drag her out of the house? What if she is not hungry? Would you tempt her to eat a piece of pie? Most likely, you would say: "No" to both questions. Yet, ignoring our body's messages, we drag ourselves out of the house when ill and eat when we are not hungry.

Listening to our body can get tricky. Should you listen to it when it says it doesn't feel like exercising? Or when it says you're fat?

How do you sort out the wisdom of the body from the non-sense of our brain?

- By listening to your body, I mean pay attention to the *visceral* reaction you are experiencing, not the thoughts that your brain is generating. The brain can be a baloney-generating machine that can busily create many disturbing thoughts for you (e.g. you're fat; you'll never make it, etc.). The visceral reactions, on the other hand, are like the rumblings in the stomach, or feeling so angry you can taste the bile, or shaking out of anxiety, etc. Listen to feelings in the body, not thoughts up in the head.

- Be a good friend and listen to the wisdom of your body as it speaks to you through symptoms during the day and via dreams at night—not through ruminating thoughts.

9. Fire the Dictator

I have talked to numerous women who work long hours and say although they enjoy their jobs, but can't seem to keep a balance between work, home, and leisure. These are professional women who are driven to perfection both at home and at work. They could be attorneys who can't turn down a case; psychologists who can't refuse the next evaluation; massage therapist whose weekends and weekdays have blended into one seamless week.

These women realize that this lifestyle is not healthy for them, but can't seem to control the compulsion that is driving them. After all, it is quite reinforcing to get paid and feel needed and respected in the workplace. It is not easy to stop a reinforcing habit.

- Ask yourself: "What would I do with my time and life if I wasn't working so much?" Many women do not know the answer or would feel lost. The vacuum is scary to them, so they continue to fill it with work.

- Next question is, "Is there something wrong with doing something that you are good at?" No, not a thing. However, you need to know whether the force that is driving you is the voice of <u>desire</u>, or the voice of a <u>dictator</u>. For instance, I love a clean home. When I clean my house, it is out of desire, not a response to a dictator's voice standing over me with a whip. Similarly, as you work long hours, ask yourself in an honest way, "Who is driving me to work so hard?" "Who is pleased with me when I work so hard?"

10. Appreciate Yourself

Many women spend their precious time feeling resentful toward their mates and children for not appreciating them enough. The feeling of being unappreciated extends to the workplace as well. It's as if they walk around with an empty cup, expecting others to fill it with appreciation. It may never happen.

- Be a good friend and start noticing the small things that you do everyday. As you finish a task, step back and simply acknowledge that you did it. Tell yourself: "Breakfast is made. Children have a nutritious meal", "I drove everyone safely to school", "and I prepared a good lesson today."

- If *you* don't fill your cup, no one can, and you'll continue to be thirsty for compliments and needy for attention from others. Fill your own cup and see how wonderful it tastes.

- Before going to sleep, have a brief pillow talk with yourself and say: "You worked hard today, Julia. Thank you for everything you did. You deserve a good night's rest." Exhale deeply and go to sleep!

11. Forgive Yourself

All of us either feel guilty about something we have done or regret something we haven't done in our lives. Guilt can choke our growth and lead to depression. But that doesn't stop us from feeling it year after year.

- Perhaps talking to the person whom you have hurt would help improve the situation now, consider it carefully and proceed. Speak from the heart; ask for forgiveness, and whether he/she forgives you, you have done your best.

- Maybe you feel you cannot talk to the person about the past. There comes a time when you need to forgive yourself. Draw a line in the sand and stop the torture.

- Mothers: Listen. You are going to become the primary target for what is wrong with your adult children. You didn't do enough of this or that or the other. If you take all of their complaints personally, the burden of guilt will be so heavy that you cannot walk. You need to take appropriate responsibility for your part, but to be fair to yourself, draw the line and tell yourself: *"I did*

the best that I could with the knowledge that I had at the time as their
mother."

Treat yourself as you would treat others.

That's our new Golden Rule.

References

Listing references that have contributed to this book is difficult for me; it is like asking a honeybee to count for the contribution that each flower has made to its honey. How does a bee really know?

We read books, listen to music, talk to others, and never know which word or piece of information makes us grow or even when the growth happens. Nonetheless, it is customary to list books as references. Here are some of the books that I have enjoyed and learned from over the years. I am sure they have contributed to my perspective in writing this book. But, these are only books. There are many conversations, mentors, songs, poems, dreams, movies, sites around the world, and other contributing factors that do not lend themselves neatly into a reference list. They too deserve to be acknowledged.

Beck, J.C. (1989). Everyday Zen: Love & Work, New York: Harper Collins

Beck, J.C. (1993). Nothing Special: Living Zen, San Francisco: Harper Collins

Bender, S. (1989). Plain and Simple: A Woman's Journey to the Amish, New York: Harper Collins

Dawkins, R. (2006). 30th Edition. The selfish gene, Oxford: University Press

Ghareman, A. (2003). *Soul of Word, Soul of World: Persian Poets Make an Offering to the west.* San Luis Obispo: Mazda Connections.

Ghareman, A. (2005). *Longing for a Land: The Story of A Persian Woman's Individuation in America.* San Luis Obispo: Mazda Connections.

Haley J. (1973) *Uncommon Therapy: The Psychiatric Techniques of Milton H. Erickson, MD.* New York: Norton

Hillman, J. (1976). *Re-Visioning Psychology.* New York: Harper Perennial

Persons J. (1989). *Cognitive Therapy in Practice: A Case Formulation Approach.* New York: Norton

Pinker, S. (2002). *The Blank Slate: The Modern Denial of Human Nature.* New York: Viking

Schnarch, D. (1997). *Passionate Marriage.* New York: Owl Books

Segal H. (1974). 2nd Edition. *Introduction to the Work of Melanie Klein.* Basic Books

Singer, J. (1994). *Boundaries of the Soul: The practice of Jung's psychology.* New York: Doubleday

Stein, M. (1982). *Jungian Analysis,* 2nd Edition. Chicago and La Salle: Open Court

Woodman, M. (1982). *Addiction to Perfection: The Still Unravished Bride.* Toronto: Inner City Books

Acknowledgement

Anne D'Arcy, Janet Lorenzo, and Judy Abbott: I am grateful that you read my manuscript and provided constructive feedback to me.

Special thanks to Dr. Jan Simek and my daughter Roshan for helping with the cover design and photography.

Thank you all for your generous support and friendship!

ORDER FORM

Use this form to order additional copies of *Six Life Secrets of Content Women*
or visit **www.mazdaconnections.com**

Please Print:

Name ....

Address ....

City .... State ....

e-mail (optional) ....

_____ copies of book @ $13.95 each   _____

_____ Postage @ $2.40 for 1st copy   _____

       add 45c for additional copies ordered to *same* address   _____

_____ CA residents add $1.22 tax per book   _____

Total amount enclosed $ _____

Make checks payable to: **Mazda Connections**

Mail to: **Mazda Connections**
1241 Johnson Avenue, PMB 118
San Luis Obispo, CA 93401-3306

Please allow 1-2 weeks for delivery.